D1599992

I'M
SPIRITUAL
NOT
RELIGIOUS

DAVID COOPER

Unless otherwise noted, Scripture quotations are taken from the *Holy Bible, New International Version®. NIV®* Copyright © 1973, 1978, 1984 by International Bible Society. Used by permission of Zondervan Publishing House. All rights reserved.

Scripture quotations marked *KJV* are taken from the King James Version of the Bible.

Scripture quotations marked *NASB* are taken from the *New American Standard Bible®.* Copyright © The Lockman Foundation 1960, 1962, 1963, 1968, 1971, 1972, 1973, 1975, 1977, 1995. Used by permission.

Scripture quotations marked *NKJV* are taken from the *New King James Version.* Copyright © 1979, 1980, 1982, 1990, 1995, Thomas Nelson, Inc., Publishers.

Scripture quotations marked *NLT* are taken from the *Holy Bible, New Living Translation,* copyright © 1996, 2004, 2007, 2012. Used by permission of Tyndale House Publishers, Inc., Wheaton, Illinois 60189. All rights reserved.

Book Editor: Lance Colkmire
Editorial Assistant: Tammy Hatfield
Copy Editor: Esther Metaxas
Technical Design: R. Ariel Vázquez

ISBN: 978-1-59684-860-3

Pathway

Copyright © 2015 by Pathway Press
1080 Montgomery Avenue
Cleveland, Tennessee 37311

All rights reserved. No part of this publication may be reproduced or transmitted in any form or by any means, electronic or mechanical, including photocopying, recording, or otherwise, or by any information storage or retrieval system, without the permission in writing from the publisher. Please direct inquiries to Pathway Press, 1080 Montgomery Avenue, Cleveland, TN 37311.

Visit *www.pathwaypress.org* for more information.

Printed in the United States of America

DEDICATION

*This book is dedicated to my wife, Barbie,
for her unwavering support of my ministry.*

CONTENTS

I'M SPIRITUAL, NOT RELIGIOUS

Sprite (the beverage) once used the slogan, "Image is nothing. Thirst is everything. Obey your thirst." Ours is a day when image is highly valued. Marketing strategies drive the sales of goods and services almost exclusively on images. The media tells us what to think, what music is cool, what movies to see, and what restaurants to visit. Sometimes we believe what we see and hear through advertisements, commercials, and the media without stopping to ask whether it is true or not.

Businesses promise more than they can deliver. Religion offers hyped-up promises for abundant life without any problems, if you follow its faith formula. Politicians spin events for their political gain. Health gurus promise weight loss without exercise and diet, if we just take the right pill. Advertisers bombard us with images of the good life, but it is often not real. Just smoke and mirrors.

Now when we apply this problem to our spirituality, we have to stop and ask: Do we only have an image of spirituality, or do we have the real thing? Spirituality can be reduced to rituals, customs, and ceremonies without any true relationship to God. Maybe that is why many people are saying, "I'm spiritual, not religious." *Spirituality* means substance, while *religion* means image. Even the Bible describes people who have "a form of godliness" while "denying its power" (2 Tim. 3:5).

The words "I'm spiritual, not religious" took on new meaning for me when I was in the hospital. One of the nurses who took care of me discovered I was a minister. She brought up the subject of *spirituality*, so I asked her about her faith. She replied quickly, "I'm spiritual, but not religious."

Intrigued, I asked, "What do you mean?" She went on to tell me that she believed in God and in Jesus, and a host of other spiritual ideas, but was not into what she called "organized religion."

So I asked her, "Are you into 'unorganized religion'?"

Laughing, she said, "That's a good question. I never thought of it like that before." More and more people are saying, "I'm spiritual. I believe in God. I want to know He has a purpose for my life. I want to experience God. *But* I don't want to be religious." *Religion* is associated with structure, rigidity, tradition, formalism, and even politics. Religion seems narrow-minded, intolerant, and judgmental—and people don't want to be a part of it. But they want a relationship with God.

This is not a new problem. Part of the magnetism of Jesus was His antagonism toward religion. He was inclusive, relevant, and compassionate. He told cool stories with spiritual punch lines. He went against the grain. He openly broke established traditions that were not based on Scripture. His messages were relevant to where people were living. Yet, He spoke the truth without reservation and challenged people to make a commitment to follow Him as Lord. He was compassionate but never compromised. He loved people unconditionally yet upheld the law of God. He championed truth but rejected tradition.

You could hang out with Jesus just like you were, but you could not stay like you were. People were changed in His presence. His words were comforting yet challenging. He was tender but always truthful. He was holy but kept company with sinners. He spoke of a world to come, yet He was at home in this present world. He was wise but talked in street language so everyone could understand Him. He possessed great power but was gentle. He was perfect but patient with others. He had great authority but He served us. *He was spiritual but not religious.*

Paul the apostle was a very religious person. Before he met Jesus, he too saw spirituality as more of a religion than a personal relationship with God. He made a big deal about observing holy days, established prayer times, man-made rules, and religious ceremonies. The day he met Jesus face-to-face changed all that. Once he met Jesus and decided to follow him, Paul's life turned 180 in the opposite direction. He went from being religious to experiencing a relationship with God. Once Jesus was Lord of his life, Paul talked more about grace than law; more about the inner life than external rules; more about unconditional love of God than self-righteous works.

Paul discovered a new purpose for life: "For to me, to live is Christ" (Phil. 1:21). Instead of wanting to know more about religion, he simply said, "I want to know Christ" (3:10). Religion had given way to a relationship with God and with the risen Lord himself. He didn't just worship God; he now walked with Him! He didn't just know *about* God; Paul knew *Him* personally.

When we read Paul's letters in the New Testament, we see an interesting development. He starts off his writings calling himself an "apostle." Later on he calls himself a "servant" of the Lord

Jesus Christ, "a prisoner of the Lord," and "the least of all God's people." Then he calls himself "the least of the apostles." In his final letters to Timothy, his son in the faith, he calls himself "the worst of sinners." He matured in humility. Even John the Baptist said of Jesus, "He must increase, but I must decrease" (John 3:30 KJV). Religion makes people proud. Spirituality makes us humble, gentle, and grateful for the amazing grace of God.

Religious people like titles of honor and public praise. When we are spiritual (not religious), we will live the secret life of discipleship. We won't need to show off our spirituality. We will avoid grandstanding. We can live without flattery. As we grow in our faith, we are either going to become more spiritual with a closer relationship with God or we will become more religious. Paul started out as a legalistic Pharisee but became the apostle of grace. Some people start out in grace and become Pharisees. That's not spiritual evolution, it's spiritual devolution!

SUBSTANCE OR STYLE?

Religion deals with style, while *spirituality* is about *substance*. Religion focuses on *what* we do, while spirituality focuses on *why* we do it. Religion is concerned with the *manner* in which something is done, while spirituality is concerned with the *motive* behind it. Even God says He searches our hearts and our minds. It is not the ritual but the reality that counts.

When I was about eight years old, I started playing drums. I had a friend who had a small starter drum set and I went to his house to play his drums while he played the organ. (He was taking lessons and became a great organist.) For Christmas that year, I wanted a drum set. My father said he could afford a certain amount and gave me two options. I could either get the sparkled blue set I found in the Sears Christmas catalog or he could buy a used Ludwig set that had less drums and cymbals and I would have to add more on my birthday and next Christmas. He told me how much better quality the Ludwig drums were than the set from Sears. I was a kid and enamored by the sparkled blue set, so that's what I got. Several years later, I regretted that decision because I realized I had chosen style over substance.

My father was an engineer and I was an artist, so our temperaments were opposite. One time he told me that I was focused on the way things looked, while he was focused on the way things worked. You can afford to be more impressed by style rather than substance when it comes to fashion, art, and even a sparkled blue drum set! But you cannot afford to be influenced by style when it comes to spirituality. You need the real thing!

We are taught the importance of substance over style in the story of the anointing of young David to be the king of Israel. The name *David* appears more times in the Bible than any other name—600 times in the Old Testament and 60 in the New Testament. (I like that because I can always find a scripture that speaks directly to me!) We can only imagine the feelings of David's father, Jesse, when the prophet Samuel showed up at his house in Bethlehem and told him he had come to anoint the next king of Israel. As a father he had to have been proud, anxious, curious, and overwhelmed by Samuel's words. *Why me? Why my family? Which one of my sons will God choose?*

Starting with the oldest, Jesse had his sons present themselves to Samuel. When Samuel saw his oldest son Eliab, he said to himself, *Surely this is the Lord's anointed!* But the Lord spoke to Samuel, "Do not consider his appearance or his height, for I have rejected him. The Lord does not look at the things man looks at. Man looks at the outward appearance, but the Lord looks at the heart" (1 Sam. 16:7).

Wow! Even Samuel the prophet was misled by what he saw. He too was about to choose style over substance. He was impressed by Eliab's stature and appearance. He assumed on the sheer basis of what he saw that Eliab was the Lord's choice for a new king. Three powerful truths are presented in this biblical story that we need to consider.

First, we must not make our choices based solely on first impressions. The Lord told Samuel to not even consider Eliab's stature or appearance. Things, or people, may look Christian but not be Christian at all. Charlatans and con artists use Christian language and imagery to take advantage of people all the time. Let's stop being so impressed by what we see and start looking deeper. The things that impress us do not impress God.

Second, realize we are overly focused on style, image, and appearance. We tend to look at things the wrong way, make the wrong assumptions, and draw the wrong conclusions based on what we see. We look *at* things when we should look *through* them to get down to the reality. We interpret circumstances the wrong way and overrate things that have no lasting value because we depend too much on what we see. We are misled by image. Image is not everything; reality is! We can be impressed by the style of ministry and yet be misguided by the substance—the lack of truth. Many people confuse emotion with anointing of the Holy Spirit and the work of God. It takes mental discipline to look deeper. In other words, don't buy the sparkled blue drum set!

Third, we must realize the Lord looks at the heart. The *heart* is the real person. Our heart is the center of our thoughts, passions, desires, values, and character. We cannot know our own hearts because "the heart is deceitful . . . and desperately wicked" (Jer. 17:9 NKJV). Only God can show us the true nature of things so we are not misled by what we see. David prayed, "Search me, O God, and know my heart" (Ps. 139:23). We need to pray the same prayer. We also need to ask God to give us "a wise and discerning heart," as Solomon prayed (1 Kings 3:12). Only then we will have the wisdom to start choosing substance over style.

Young David was the last son to come before Samuel. He was a singer/songwriter who took care of his daddy's sheep. His own father didn't think David had what it took to be chosen. That is why Jesse never even presented David to Samuel. David was out in the field working and was not even invited in so Samuel could meet him. After Samuel met all of Jesse's seven other sons and the Lord let him know none of them was to be king, Samuel had to ask Jesse if he had any more sons! Talk about nobody believing in you.

"There is still the youngest . . . but he is tending the sheep" (1 Sam. 16:11), Jesse told Samuel. Listen to the implication: There is still the youngest, *but* . . . he is too young . . . he has his head in the clouds composing music . . . he is not as physically fit as the others. But, but, but . . .

"Send for him; we will not sit down until he arrives" (v. 11). Samuel made everybody stand up and wait for David. Finally, young David walked in the house, dirty and sweaty from working with the sheep. As soon as Samuel laid eyes on him, the Lord spoke to his heart: "Rise and anoint him; he is the one!" (v. 12). Truly, God's ways are not our ways, and His thoughts are higher than ours. It is the substance (not the style) that matters.

Recently, I spoke with a young man when he attended our church for the first time. He said he had heard about our ministry and was glad to finally get a chance to attend a worship service. He said he was deeply moved by the worship and the teaching of God's Word. "I wasn't sure what to expect when I came to a mega-church," he said. "I expected a large church to be more focused on the style rather than on substance. I have been so touched today by the substance of the message you preached. God did a great work in my life today through this time of worship."

CHECK YOUR BAGGAGE

The early Christian churches we read about in the New Testament were made up of people from different religious backgrounds. They were Orthodox Jews, Greeks, and Romans, while others came from Eastern religions. Some had no religious background at all. They had to leave their religions and cultures behind in order to find unity as believers in Jesus.

We stand equal at the foot of the cross of Jesus. We follow Him as Lord and have to leave our religious baggage behind when we enter the kingdom of God. Religious and cultural baggage dilutes the Christian faith, making it something less than fully Christian. Not all aspects of what is often presented as Christianity are actually Christian. It is not like Jesus, or anything like what Jesus said or did. Many Christian traditions have little or nothing to do with Jesus. We need to "throw off everything that . . . entangles [us]" so that we can "run with perseverance the race marked out for us" as we "fix our eyes on Jesus, the author and perfecter of our faith" (Heb. 12:1-2).

Many Jewish leaders became followers of Jesus in the early days of the Christian faith. They came from different sects of Judaism. Men like Paul and Nicodemus were Pharisees. Others, like Barnabas, were Levitical priests, many of whom were Sadducees. The Sadducees were liberal, while the Pharisees were hyper-conservative. Others were from the strictest sect of all—the Essenes, who left Judea to build a community in the desert. They thought they were the true people of God and that everybody else was wrong. The community they built to withdraw from society is the place where the Dead Sea Scrolls were discovered in 1947. They devoted themselves to copying Scriptures and other religious writings. At first they said they were so spiritual, they would not let their wives live with them. They put their wives and children in a nearby village when they devoted themselves to copying sacred texts. But that didn't last long. They quickly discovered they needed the women and brought everyone together.

All these groups had different theological ideas about Judaism. When many of them accepted Jesus as Messiah and became the first Christians, they had different views of what it meant to be a Christian. They made the mistake of bringing their religious views, traditions, customs, and rules into the Christian faith. They ended up divided and arguing about whose traditions ought to be followed by all Christians. One of the issues Paul often faced were the Pharisees who opposed his message of salvation by grace alone. They wanted to make Jewish customs mandatory for everyone who became a follower of Jesus.

TRUTH OR TRADITION?

Are we going to follow religious traditions or the biblical truth? When Paul and Barnabas finished their missionary trip, they presented a progress report to the apostles in Jerusalem. This led to discussion and debate among the apostles about what Paul and Barnabas were supposed to preach in regard to salvation by grace through faith and what it means to be a Christian. After listening to all the issues, the apostles passed a ruling that all people are saved by grace through faith in Jesus Christ alone, and that Gentile believers were not obligated to follow Jewish customs (see Acts 15).

This issue has been our struggle for two thousand years! Certain groups and denominations want to tell everybody what it means to be a Christian . . . and if we don't meet their standards, live up to their rules, hold their view, or meet their test of faith, they have the audacity to tell us we are not truly Christian. But you cannot add anything to the grace of God. Paul declared, "By the grace of God I am what I am" (1 Cor. 15:10).

Paul dealt with this issue head-on when he wrote to the Colossians, "My purpose [in writing this letter] is that [you] may be encouraged in heart and united in love, so that [you] may have the full riches of complete understanding, in order that [you] may know the mystery of God, namely, Christ" (2:2). He defined "the mystery of God" as the plan of salvation through Jesus Christ ordained since the beginning of the world (see 1:26-27). God sent a Person, His Son—not a set of principles, a set of ideas, or a doctrinal creed—to save the world from sin.

There is a big difference between following a person and following a philosophy. Jesus said, "Follow Me." He didn't say, "Follow My ideas," or "Follow My principles." He didn't even say, "Follow My followers." He simply said, "Follow Me." The teachings of Jesus found in the Gospels of Matthew, Mark, Luke, and John are explained and applied in the other New Testament letters by the apostles.

John the apostle described *spirituality* in personal terms: "The Word [Jesus] became flesh and made his dwelling among us" (John 1:14). God appeared to us in a Person, His only Son, Jesus. *Christianity* is not a set of principles, ideas, or laws; it is a Person.

A *Christian* is a person who has a personal relationship with Jesus through faith—plain and simple. Nothing more, nothing less. Jesus came to show us His love by saving us from our sins so we might have everlasting life. *Spirituality* is knowing Him! It is not about belonging to some particular group of Christians and living by their prescribed traditions. Jesus prayed, "This is eternal life: that they may know you, the only true God, and Jesus Christ, whom you have sent" (17:3).

The joy of being a Christian comes from a simple faith that trusts Jesus completely for salvation. "Though you have not seen him, you love him; and even though you do not see him now, you believe in him and are filled with an inexpressible and glorious joy" (1 Peter 1:8). Joy comes from loving Him and believing in Him, not in following religious traditions and man-made rules. His way is "easy and [His] burden is light" (Matt. 11:30). The way of religion is hard and difficult and makes us feel like we never add up. His way fills us with joy unspeakable.

IT'S NOT WHAT YOU KNOW BUT WHO YOU KNOW

Gnostic philosophers corrupted the Christian faith in the early days of the movement. The apostle Paul dealt with their errors when he wrote Colossians. The word *gnostic* comes from the Greek word *gnosis*, meaning "knowledge." They thought they knew everything! Knowledge was their big claim to fame.

They knew everything and no one else knew anything, as far as they were concerned. The Gnostics are still with us! They claimed to have a deep, hidden, secret spiritual knowledge that only the elite possess. They talked about higher revelation, hidden knowledge, and deep secrets.

Paul confronted their error by saying, "In [Christ] are hidden all the treasures of wisdom and knowledge" (Col. 2:3). If you have Jesus, you have the knowledge of God. *All* the treasures of knowledge—not *some* of them or even *most* of them—are hidden in Christ. Once you have Him, you are filled with wisdom and knowledge. The Gnostics were adding philosophy to faith in Jesus in the same way the religious leaders were adding their traditions to faith in Jesus. Some added *law* to grace and *works* to faith instead of keeping it simple: we are saved "by grace . . . through faith" (Eph. 2:8) period.

Being *spiritual* is having a personal relationship with Jesus. This is what Paul means when he writes, "So then, just as you received Christ Jesus as Lord, continue to live in him" (Col. 2:6). Have you received and welcomed Jesus into your life? Do you remember when you received Jesus as your Savior? Do you remember how simple and pure that moment of faith began in your life? Well, keep it like that! Don't let people like the Gnostics make it complicated for you. "Continue to live in him" means to continue in your faith and devotion to Jesus. If you're not careful, you can get off course and fall into the trap of religion. Paul knew by personal experience that the real impediment to a relationship with Jesus is getting bogged down in religious traditions.

A little girl was seeing her pediatrician for a cold. He put the otoscope in her ear, looked around, and said, "Do you think I will find Big Bird in there?" She sat silent.

Then he took his tongue depressor, inserted it in her mouth to look at her throat. "Do you think I will find the Cookie Monster down there?" She just sat there silent.

He then took his stethoscope and put it to her chest to listen to her heart. He said, "Do you think I will find Barney in your heart?"

She said, "Oh no, sir. Jesus is in my heart. Barney is on my underpants."

It is who is in your heart that matters! Continue to live *in Him*— not in the complications of religious traditions, customs, or rules.

We run the risk of getting away from our relationship to the Lord and falling into the pit of religion. "Prone to wander, Lord, I feel it, prone to leave the God I love," wrote Robert Robinson. We don't just wander off into sin; sometimes we wander off into legalism or weird spirituality instead of being satisfied with Jesus. I like the song "Jesus Is All I Need." That says it best for me. How about you?

As Paul seeks to keep from wandering from the truth, he writes: "See to it that no one takes you captive through hollow and deceptive philosophy, which depends on human tradition and the basic principles of this world rather than on Christ. For in Christ all the fullness of the Deity lives in bodily form, and you have been given fullness in Christ, who is the head over every power and authority" (Col. 2:8-10).

Think about that statement and take it to heart: "See to it that no one takes you captive through hollow and deceptive philosophy." The word *captive* means to be put in bondage and to lose our freedom. There are people who will make you the prisoner of their traditions, opinions, and personal convictions if you let them—so don't let them!

He says, "see to it" that no one takes you captive. If you are not aware of the dangers of religion, you will find yourself drifting away from your relationship with the Lord and falling into captivity to religion and legalism. He is not talking here about being captive to sin but captive to religion, which he calls "empty philosophies and high-sounding nonsense that come from human thinking and from the spiritual powers of this world, rather than from Christ" (v. 8 NLT).

LIGHTEN UP

A friend of mine named his boat *Lighten Up!* Every time I have the opportunity to get on that boat, it reminds me to unwind, lighten up, and enjoy my vacation.

In another sense, Paul tells us to lighten up in Galatians 5:1: "It is for freedom that Christ has set us free. Stand firm, then, and do not let yourselves be burdened again by a yoke of slavery." This is one of my favorite statements in the Bible: Stand firm in freedom. Religion is hard and burdensome, but following Jesus is easy and light. The "yoke of slavery" means slavery to religious rules and customs that are not taught in Scripture. We can be slaves to people's opinions, church creeds, and religious rituals if we don't stand firm in our freedom. We can be taken captive by the false idea that we have to earn our salvation, or to add to the grace of God by good works instead of trusting Christ alone to give us eternal life.

Obviously, sin is a type of bondage and only Jesus can free us from it. But religion is another form of bondage from which Jesus came to free us. When Jesus said, "Come to me, all you who are weary and burdened" (Matt. 11:28), He was talking about the burden of religion the Pharisees had placed on people. Judaism began as a religion of love, but they turned it into a religion of law. Jesus called people who were burdened with religion and said, "Take my yoke upon you . . . and you will find rest for your souls. For my yoke is easy and my burden is light" (vv. 29-30).

The word *yoke* stands out. Paul talked about religion as a "yoke of slavery," and Jesus spoke of it as a "heavy burden." Jesus says if we believe in Him, He would give us a yoke that is easy, a burden that is light and rest for our souls. Many people are burned out on religion. Religion is heavy. It is hard to keep all the rules, to maintain a holier-than-thou image when you know the truth about yourself. It is hard trying to be perfect to get to heaven. But when you trust Jesus as your Savior you let go of the heavy yoke of sin and religion and you put on His yoke that is easy. That means you team up with Him; you share the yoke with Him; you don't carry it alone. You enjoy a life filled with purpose, power, and peace that will lead to heaven! He gives rest to your soul. Religion, on the other hand, will keep you tied up in knots worrying about your relationship with God and wondering whether or not you will make it to heaven.

Take charge of your life and don't let other people live your faith for you. You have to think for yourself. You don't have to believe everything proclaimed in the Lord's name. Remember, "Many false prophets have gone out into the world" (1 John 4:1). Sometimes they are well-meaning people who are just misguided or immature. Other times they are false prophets intentionally, leading people astray. Some people want to feel important, so they set themselves up as spiritual mentors looking for somebody to depend on them for spiritual guidance. Even churches can be overbearing, trying to control everything people think and do with a long list of rules and regulations until every ounce of personal expression and individual thought is stamped out. We end up mindless, repeating the creeds, following the protocol, and acting like clones instead of being the unique individuals God created us to be. Don't let that happen to you. Think for yourself. Pray to God directly about decisions and listen to the voice of the Holy Spirit. Read the Bible for yourself to hear from God. "See to it that no one takes you captive" (Col. 2:8), but stand firm in the freedom Jesus Christ has given you.

It has been said, "The price of freedom is eternal vigilance." You have to guard your freedom because some will put you in bondage to their rules and personal beliefs. Don't let people take you captive by hollow and deceptive philosophy and religious traditions. Some people are on a power trip in their family, in businesses, in politics, in the media, in education and, yes, even in religion; and they will tell you how to think, feel, and act. They will take you captive by getting you to believe their hollow and deceptive ideas that are based on their views rather than on Scripture.

So, "be on your guard so that you may not be carried away by the error of lawless men and fall from your secure position. But grow in the grace and knowledge of our Lord and Savior Jesus Christ" (2 Peter 3:17-18). You must guard your heart and mind against hollow and deceptive philosophy so that you can grow in your personal relationship with Jesus. Don't be taken captive by other people's opinions. Instead, "take captive every thought to make it obedient to Christ" (2 Cor. 10:5).

A CASE FOR COMMON SENSE

A lack of open and honest discussion exists among Christians these days. Many Bible studies are nothing more than one person presenting the material and everyone else listening without asking questions, sharing their views, or discussing real-life issues. Sometimes we don't ask questions or give our personal views because we're afraid people will criticize us for not following the group consensus. I encourage you to ask the questions. Point out contradictions when you see them. Challenge the status quo. Accept the Bible as the final authority over every idea, principle, or law.

You have the right to think for yourself and have your own views of how the Word of God applies to you. This is especially true when the answers people are giving do not add up. Barbie and I had dinner with a pastor and his wife whose twenty-six-year-old son was killed in a car crash. They are thinking about giving up the ministry because of the grief they still battle. We were talking over dinner about how spiritual clichés in times of tragedy do more harm than good. They told me of receiving friends at the funeral and people saying foolish things like, "God just wanted another member in His choir," or "God needed him more in heaven than you do." While people may mean well, the words hurt them deeply and, worse, angered them.

Our faith is more than meaningless clichés. This couple got so tired of people misquoting or misapplying Paul's famous statement in Romans 8:28, "In all things God works for the good of those who love him." People often say all *things* work together for good. No, they don't. Things don't work at all. Things are the events of life that happen, both good and bad. It is *God who works for our good*, in spite of what happens to us. That is what Paul is saying to us. There is nothing good about parents losing their son in a fatal automobile crash. A car wreck is bad, sickness is bad, divorce is bad, and bankruptcy is bad. These things are not good, and they don't produce anything good.

God is good! We can experience the goodness of God in a world where bad things happen. The goodness of God's grace sustains us. The goodness of His power upholds us. The goodness of His love assures us. The goodness of His presence guides us.

Paul the apostle is not saying that everything that happens to us is good. He is saying that in spite of everything that happens to us, God is good and He works in everything for our good!

Some people say God has a purpose in everything. No, He does not—not in everything *we* do. He has a purpose in everything *He* does. He "works out everything in conformity with the purpose of his will" (Eph. 1:11). Many of the things you and I do have no eternal purpose. Think of all the foolish and sinful things done in this world that bring so much harm. We are responsible to God for our actions. We need to stop ascribing to God the collateral damage of our actions. We need to know the difference between what we are doing and what God is doing.

God's actions serve His eternal purpose. Every single event that happens in the world is not His will, His work, nor His purpose. I am glad that God's purpose for us and for the history of the world will prevail over all the actions of man. I am glad that in this world where bad things happen, God is good and He is at work in the lives of those who love Him for their good. Life may be bad at times, but God is good. As the prophet declared, "The Lord is good, a refuge in times of trouble" (Nah. 1:7).

We need to know what the Scripture teaches and what it does not teach. I watched a well-known lecturer on creationism debate an evolutionist. The interviewer asked a question, and the guy who is supposed to be an expert on creationism had no real answer. He gave a pat answer that did not address the subject. He merely tried to defend his position that the universe is only 6,000 years old. The Bible does not say the universe and the earth is only 6,000 years old. It says, "In the beginning God created the heavens and the earth" (Gen. 1:1). We don't know when that occurred, and neither do scientists. But there is good evidence it is older than 6,000 years. Since God is eternal, there has to be more going on than what has taken place the last 6,000 years.

In 1927, Georges Lemaître proposed the Big Bang theory of the universe. The theory says all the matter in the universe was originally compressed into a tiny dot. In a fraction of a second, the dot expanded, and all the matter instantly filled what is now our universe. This "Big Bang" explosion marked the beginning of time.

The Big Bang theory was first published in *Physical Review* by Alpher, Bethe, and Gamow, in the April 1, 1952, issue (April Fool's Day). The Big Bang is a theory based on light travel (186,000 miles per second). Science says the universe has a definite beginning in time and space, and that from that beginning rate at which light travels from that point equates to the universe could easily be 13.7 billion years old.

Now, to my point of thinking through what you believe and making sure your beliefs make sense, the creationist on the debate could have easily connected the Big Bang theory with Genesis 1 . . . if he could have gotten off his soapbox of holding to a 6,000-year-old view of the universe. The Big Bang says the cosmos began as a catastrophic event with a definite beginning and that started with light. The theory is based on measuring the time and distance of light and matter moving away from that point of origin. That sounds like Genesis to me! God said, "Let there be light!" God started the world—He is the source of power and energy that created the cosmos—and He began it with light! Arguing about when that took place is pointless, but using science to support the Genesis claim is vital to this generation. If you think about the Genesis story, it does not sound preposterous to people today because it has the elements of an extraordinary event—time, space, matter, and light. If people say they believe in the Big Bang, then they already believe the basic truths of Creation taught in Genesis!

When you know your faith and understand the Word of God for yourself, your faith will stand in the face of all intellectual challenges. You will know what you believe as a Christian and why you believe it. You will then be able "to give an answer to everyone who asks you to give the reason for the hope that you have" (1 Peter 3:15).

A little girl's mother tried to console her daughter after her cat died. "It's O.K., sweetheart. Tabby is now with God in heaven," her mother said tenderly.

With a bewildered look on her face, she looked up at her mother and asked, "Mom, what does God want with a dead cat?"

Our answers need to make sense about what we believe as Christians. We must know what we believe and why we believe it.

Recently, I wrote a creed to express what I know as a follower of Jesus Christ. It's simply called "Creed":

I believe in God the Father; I believe in Christ His Son.
I believe in the Holy Spirit; I believe in the great three in one.
I believe in divine creation; I believe in the mystery of God.

I believe in the hosts of heaven; I believe in His everlasting love.
I believe.

I believe in the death of Jesus; I believe He atoned for our sins.
I believe in His resurrection; I believe death He destroyed.
I believe He ascended to heaven; I believe that He reigns on high.
I believe in His intercession; I believe in His power to save.
I believe.

I believe the trumpet will sound His appearing; I believe the dead in
   Christ will rise.
I believe we will meet Him in glory; I believe some will never really die.
I believe we will see His splendor; I believe every knee will bow.
I believe He's returning in power; I believe His kingdom will stand.
I believe.

I believe when the storm clouds gather; I believe when doubts assail.
I believe when the heavens are shaken; I believe when the earth
   gives way.
I believe when our hearts are fearful; I believe all things will come
   to pass.
I believe in His promise to keep us; I believe His Word will last.
I believe.

I believe in His eternal purpose; I believe in His perfect plan.
I believe He works in all things; I believe His promise will stand.
I believe I am made in His image; I believe I am shaped by His hand.
I believe I am led by His Spirit; I believe in His design so grand.
I believe.

I believe I am covered with His mercy; I believe I am safe in His hand.
I believe I am kept by His power; I believe I am loved for all time.

I believe in His abiding presence; I believe I am never alone.
I believe I will overcome life's battles; I believe in my heavenly home.
I believe.

COMPLETE IN CHRIST

I f anyone is in Christ, he is a new creation" (2 Cor. 5:17)! Paul uses the phrase "in Christ" 172 times to describe the closest relationship possible. To be *in Christ* is greater than being *near* Christ, or *believing in* Christ, or *following* Christ, or *acknowledging* Christ. I am in Christ, and Christ is in me. Being "in Christ" is more than merely believing in Jesus, hearing about Jesus, learning about Jesus, respecting Jesus, or casually following Jesus. Every moment is lived in His presence and grace. I am always mindful of Him and He is mindful of me. I have become one with Him.

To those who feel spiritually inadequate, Paul says, "In Christ all the fullness of the Deity lives in bodily form, and you have been given fullness in Christ" (Col. 2:9-10). *Fullness* means to be complete. Everything you are looking for and longing for is found in Christ. Stop looking for more spiritual experiences! That's where people get off track. You may say, "I need more fullness of joy, peace, and purpose." Spiritual fullness is found in Christ! The closer you get to Jesus and the more real He becomes to you, the more fullness of joy, peace, and purpose you'll have in your life.

CHEAP SUBSTITUTES

There are many substitutes for spirituality. These individuals have some marks of spirituality but fall short of a meaningful relationship with God. Let's give them titles so we can identify them—the ritualist, the legalist, the mystic, the universalist, the emotionalist, the motivationalist, and the materialist.

The *ritualist* practices ceremonies, attends religious services, and observes holy days but has, at best, a shallow relationship with God. Prayers are memorized mantras they repeat rather than a conversation with God. They practice religious rituals in an obsessive-compulsive fashion—doing the rituals at the same time, in the same place, in the same order. Their worship services are calculated from start to finish. Religion is very structured and organized, and once you complete the ritual, you are finished and can get on with your life.

God says to these people, "Stop bringing meaningless offerings!" (Isa. 1:13). God wants us to stop doing meaningless religious rituals. He wants us to know Him and to enjoy a relationship with Him as our heavenly Father. Even though ritualists get very little out of their spirituality, they continue to practice the rituals and attend services out of obligation and habit. God says it is meaningless both to Him and to them.

Look Out for Legalism

The *legalist* sees faith as a strict observance to laws and rules. Legalists judge themselves and others by their own standards of righteousness instead of the Word of God. This makes them feel better than other people. Jesus observed them as people who were "confident of their own righteousness and looked down on everybody else" (Luke 18:9). They treasure their traditions over the truth of God. "These people honor me with their lips, but their hearts are far from me. . . . Their teachings are but rules taught by men," Jesus said (Matt. 15:8-9).

Jesus told His disciples, "Be on your guard against the yeast of the Pharisees and Sadducees" (16:6). It only takes a small amount of yeast to work through an entire batch of dough. Just a small amount of legalism takes us away from the liberty of grace and puts us in spiritual bondage.

Legalism kills spirituality. "The letter kills, but the Spirit gives life" (2 Cor. 3:6). Paul once prided himself on being a person of "legalistic righteousness" (Phil. 3:6). Then he met Jesus face-to-face and experienced the grace of God. From that point on, he said he did not want "a righteousness of my own that comes from the law, but that which is through faith in Christ" (v. 9).

The legalist takes man-made rules, customs, religious traditions, political views, personal convictions, and opinions and adds them to the simple law of God and the grace of God. They want everyone to conform to their standards. That puts them in the place of judging people on the basis of their own opinions. Legalism has taken its toll for centuries, driving people away from Christ. Legalists make spirituality complicated as opposed to the simple grace of God. They lay down so many rules that it makes people think it is too hard to be a Christian. People feel they can never measure up to the perfectionistic standards of the legalist.

The legalist teaches traditions as though they are biblical, so people get tradition tangled up with truth. If you grew up in a legalistic environment, you may not know the difference between biblical truth and religious tradition. People believe those legalistic rules are in the Bible, but they are not. Legalists like to use the phrase "The Bible says . . . " in front of their viewpoint. But, of course, they never direct you to any passage because the Bible does not say what they claim.

If you have been the victim of legalism, then get as far away from it as you can. Legalism is toxic, spiritually and emotionally. Read the Bible for yourself and separate what is biblical from mere traditions that have been passed down for generations.

People frequently ask me where something is found in the Bible. Often I have to respond by saying, "It's not in the Bible." The look on people's faces is priceless! Not everything you've been told is in the Bible is actually in it. Many things you've heard are nothing more than religious tradition. Jesus said, "Their teachings are but rules taught by men" (Matt. 15:9).

Legalists make it hard on everyone else but easy on themselves. They are busy minding everyone else's spiritual business.

A story was told of a man who died and arrived at the pearly gates. Peter said to him, "You only have to meet one condition to enter heaven: Spell the word *love*."

The man said, "That's easy. *L-o-v-e.*"

Peter said, "I've got to run an errand. Will you watch the gate for me? Just give each person this same test until I get back." So the man took over for Peter. He greeted a few people, and then was shocked to see his wife.

"What are you doing here?" he asked.

She said, "I was in a car wreck and killed on impact."

"Well, he said," there's only one condition to get into heaven—spell *Czechoslovakia.*"

God Out of Focus

The *mystic* has a non-defined spirituality. Mystics view God as more of an impersonal force as opposed to a person—a force of life at work in nature. Some think of God as the "Force" in *Star Wars* that can be used for good or evil. God, to them, is "Mother Nature," the laws of nature itself. *Mysticism* seldom defines God as a person and never defines God as our Redeemer or as the Absolute Truth. Many people believe in a host of mystical ideas such as channeling, charms, amulets, ghosts, hauntings, crystals, pyramid power, reincarnation, and astral projection. They value their personal experiences of mystical realities more than the world they can touch, see, and feel.

The *universalist* has no boundaries of right and error, no absolute truth, and believes all roads lead to God. "It doesn't matter what you believe, as long as you're sincere in your beliefs" is their main belief. To them all religions and philosophies are the same and equally beneficial. The universalist believes everything and nothing at the same time. He or she accepts every religion and rejects the notion that one religion is better than another. They have the luxury of never making a decision about anything spiritual. Universalism is convenient for those who cannot decide what is right or wrong, true or false. The universalist does not want to decide, take a side, form an opinion, or take a stand. "To each his own," is their motto.

More Than a Feeling

Faith in Jesus Christ is more than a feeling. The *emotionalist* measures his faith by his feelings. He or she often gets caught up in spiritual hysteria and extremes. Emotionalists measure their relationship with God on the basis of how they feel. They talk about "feeling led by God," or they say, "I feel God is speaking to me." But there is a big difference between *feeling* led and actually *being* led by God. There is a big difference between feeling like God is speaking and God actually speaking to us.

I often hear people remark, "I feel like God has something really important for me to do." Rarely do they use the word *think*. They prefer the word *feel* because they basically feel their way through life. For many of them there is little, if any, place for logic in their spirituality.

They often speak of difference between knowing in your mind versus knowing in your heart. This is preposterous because the mind and the heart are the same thing. Knowing is an intellectual ability and it only takes place in the brain, the center of what we call the mind. You don't have two brains, one physical and the other spiritual. The Bible says, "As [a man] thinks in his heart, so is he" (Prov. 23:7 NKJV). The words *heart* and *mind* are used interchangeably in Scripture. (I will acknowledge that we can know something at deeper levels and have a greater knowledge of God, and this may be what we mean when we speak of "heart knowledge.")

The emotionalist believes God's main job is to make him or her feel good. "I must never feel bad about anything," is their motto. They think God has left them if they get discouraged or depressed. But if they are feeling good, they conclude God is at work! Blessings and feelings are the same thing to them. They measure everything by their emotions. However, you cannot interpret everything that is going on in the world around you by the world within you. This is an extremely limited way to measure what God is doing in our lives.

Our feelings may change, but God is the same (Ps. 102:27). Feelings come and go, rise and fall, but the Word of God remains forever (1 Peter 1:25). Emotions fluctuate as a result of chemical balances in the brain, physical conditions, diet, sleep, stress, and circumstances. Emotions don't measure anything, and we cannot count on them to guide our lives.

My father was an avid train collector. That was his only hobby. I have learned that emotions are not the "engine" that directs and pulls our lives but the "caboose" that trails along at the end of the train. The engine has all the power that pulls the cars along the track. The engine of our lives is the will that makes decisions.

When we think clearly and choose wisely, our emotions follow along and get in line.

Feelings are a reaction to what's going on in the moment, much of which none of us can even control. Emotions enrich our lives. They make us happy and miserable, peaceful and stressed out, joyful and sorrowful. But emotions are followers, not leaders. We get in trouble when we let our feelings lead us instead of thinking things through. It is a big mistake to make emotions the barometer of our relationship to God. Faith is based on eternal truth, not on emotional tangents! When you are feeling down, remember that your faith rests on God's eternal truth, not your temporary emotions!

Early in my ministry I spoke at a revival service. The service was so hyped up that I could not wait to leave. When I got into my car I prayed just so I could sense the presence of the Lord, because in that service I felt a million miles away from God. There was a lot of noise and emotionalism, but not anything that seemed spiritual to me. I could not wait to leave church so I could sense God's presence again! It was just like Paul's comment, "If I speak in the tongues of men and of angels, but have not love, I am only a resounding gong or a clanging cymbal" (1 Cor. 13:1). That gathering was more of a "resounding gong" than it was a true worship experience. Paul even told the Corinthians that their worship services did more harm than good!

More Than a Motivational Talk

The *motivationalist* thinks of spirituality as pop-psychology or a self-help program. To them there is little difference between prosperity-gospel broadcast and the Oprah Winfrey Network. They just want a positive message of self-help. They want preachers to be motivational speakers, to make them feel good, to believe they can achieve anything! They don't want ministers to preach the gospel of Christ, or the way of salvation, or the truth of God to teach them how to live. They are uncomfortable with talk about right and wrong, righteousness and sin, and prefer to take the high ground of positive thinking and avoid such controversial subjects as "truth."

I am not casting aspersions on positive thinking—I am all for it. It is a lot better than negative thinking! But there is more to life and to our relationship to God than just positive thinking. You can be an atheist but think positively. So, positive thinking alone is not going to satisfy your need of a relationship with God. Preaching is greater than giving a motivational talk, even though the Word of God motivates us. But God's Word also challenges us, stretches us, convicts us, confronts us, reassures us, and transforms us by the renewing of our minds. The purpose of relationship with God is greater than God making us feel good. It is also about knowing the truth that sets us free. Jesus said, "If you hold to my teaching, you are really my disciples. Then you will know the truth, and the truth will set you free" (John 8:31-32).

True Riches

The *materialist* views faith and spirituality as an in-road to a better life economically and materially. They mistakenly "think that godliness is a means to financial gain" (1 Tim. 6:5). They look for the temporal return on their faith and de-emphasize eternal matters. They believe the proof of faith and the blessings of God is financial security, good health, and a successful life.

The materialist ignores statements like James 2:5: "Has God not chosen the poor of this world to be rich in faith?" (NKJV). They would say that is impossible. According to their logic, if you are rich in faith, you will be rich materially. But that is not always the case. God does promise to provide for our needs, but we are also subject in part to the economy of the nation where we live.

Wealth is drastically different in a democratic nation like America than a totalitarian country under a dictator. Christians all over the world have different economic levels based partly on the economy of where they live. We are affected by both national and global economies. The Bible does not teach that if you become more spiritual, you will get richer financially. In fact, one of the great marks of true spirituality is to give your money away and not keep it all for yourself. Jesus said, "It is more blessed to give than to receive" (Acts 20:35). Real spirituality is measured by how much you give away, not by how much you accumulate. You get richer in other ways. God does promise to bless us and provide financially, and He is faithful to do so. But He has even greater riches for us.

One guy believed he could take his money with him when he died. He prayed and the Lord granted his request, but with one stipulation—he could bring only one suitcase filled with money. He decided to fill the case with gold bricks. The day came when he died. An angel greeted him at the gates of heaven but told him he couldn't bring his suitcase into heaven. "But I have an agreement with God," the man protested.

"That's unusual," said the angel. "Mind if I take a look?"

The man opened the suitcase to reveal the gold.

The angel asked, "Why in the world would you bring pavement?"

Materialists make the mistake of measuring spirituality in terms of what they can touch, see, and feel. They tell themselves if everything is going great, their income is good, their investments are sound, and they are physically healthy, that means they are blessed. And those are signs of God's blessings, but that is not the whole story. They think, *If I lose my job or my business goes sour or I get sick, then God has removed His blessings from my life.* However, God is with us in the good times and the bad! He is with us in the victories and the defeats!

People play mind games with themselves when they are going through difficulties, which only make life harder. Life moves in seasons, and you are going to go through some tough times. If you tell yourself that the only measure of God's love is your material possessions, pleasant circumstances, and physical health, then you are headed for a crisis of faith when you meet tough times. You are going to crash and burn spiritually, thinking that God does not love you and He is not faithful, all because your world is not perfect.

The Old Testament account of Job is the story of a man who trusted God in good times and bad times. That is the secret of his survival. He kept his relationship with God separate from his material possessions. He was very wealthy, but he lost it all for a season. Yet, he praised God with the same fervor in the bad times as he did when everything was going great: "The Lord gave, and the Lord has taken away; blessed be the name of the Lord. . . . Though [God] slay me, yet will I trust Him" (Job 1:21; 13:15 NKJV).

God turned Job's situation around eventually and blessed him with twice as much as he had before. And the Lord will turn our situations around if we trust Him, but that doesn't mean we won't ever face difficulties. God is greater than anything we face, and He will lead us through the valley to a new place of blessing. Don't make the mistake of measuring your relationship with God on the basis of your material possessions, outward circumstances, or physical health. The Lord is with you through all the seasons of life and will give you the grace to handle life, whether it is pleasant or painful.

GOING ON A WALK WITH GOD

What does it mean to you to be spiritual and to have a close relationship with God? What kind of relationship do you want with the Lord? You have to clearly define that relationship if you want to experience it. Maybe you are tired of just being religious and want more. Then decide that you are going to stop going through the motions of religion and you are going to seek after God with all your heart. God promises, "If you seek Me you will find Me when you search for Me with all your heart" (see Jer. 29:13). But you must give up your religious traditions to have the relationship you want. You cannot have both because they are diametrically opposed to one another.

All goals start with a clear definition which, in turn, gives us direction. People lack direction because they haven't clearly defined where they want to go. So, let's define what it means to be *spiritual*. If you say, "I'm spiritual, not religious," you may be thinking more of what you don't want to be rather than what you actually want from your relationship to God.

The root of the word *spiritual* is *spirit*. The Hebrew word for *spirit* is *ruach* and first appears in Genesis 2:7: "The Lord God . . . breathed into his nostrils the breath of life [*ruach*], and the man became a living being." The story goes on to say that God walked with Adam and Eve in the "cool [*ruach*] of the day" in the Garden of Eden (3:8). The word *cool* doesn't refer to the temperature but to their unbroken spiritual relationship. When Adam and Eve rebelled against God, their relationship with Him was damaged. God reached out to Adam and Eve by His amazing grace so that their relationship was not completely destroyed, and He does the same for us.

The statement "God breathed . . . the breath of life" is a simple, pure definition of spirituality. The word *ruach* is used in Hebrew for four words—*spirit, wind, breath,* and *life*. When God made us, He made us in His image, with the breath of life, so we are different from the animal kingdom. We have His breath, His spirit within us, which is our spiritual connection with God. We are conscious of God, we have His law written on our hearts, we have a conscience and a sense of right and wrong, and we intuitively desire to worship God.

God and Adam walked together in Eden. They didn't study together, they walked. Adam didn't research the dynamics of the Divinity, trying to analyze God; instead, he walked with God. Adam didn't build temples and religious icons, he walked with God. He talked and listened to God. He had meaningful conversations with Him. He enjoyed God's presence. That is spirituality.

Is that the relationship you have with God? Is that the relationship you want? You must move beyond religious ritualism and spiritual substitutes and start going on walks with God.

God sent His Son, Jesus, into this world to pay the penalty for our sins so we might be forgiven. He came to completely restore our relationship. He sent us the Holy Spirit to live within us so that we can enjoy the presence of God. Although we don't have the Garden of Eden, we can still walk with God in the "cool of the day."

IT'S THE RELATIONSHIP!

The 1992 Clinton presidential campaign coined the phrase, "It's the economy, stupid!" Bill Clinton's campaign manager knew that elections are about the economy, so that's where he put his focus. President George Bush didn't get it and lost an election when pundits thought he was unbeatable.

Well, real spirituality is about relationships! It's the relationship that counts. Religious acts alone make us feel distant and detached from God. We feel like we're just part of a religious organization. But when we are relational and conversational, we experience His presence. James says, "Come near to God and he will come near to you" (James 4:8).

When you pray, do you talk and listen to God? Or do you read poetry, cite memorized prayers, or repeat mantras? Are you really talking with God, and do you listen to His still, small voice within your heart? When you read the Bible, do you read it as the history of God's Word in the world *and* as His personal letter to you? Or do you just study the Bible like you do a textbook on economics, history, or math? Begin to relate to God on a personal level and you will experience His nearness. You too can walk with God.

THE REAL YOU

God has made us with a spirit, a mind, and a body. You are an eternal spirit who lives in a temporary body. The apostle Paul called the physical body a "tent" that we will one day lay aside to enjoy our permanent home in heaven (2 Cor. 5:1).

Just as there is a difference between your house and your family that lives in the house, there is a difference between the real you and your body. A house becomes a home when people live inside the house. One day the house (your body) is going to wear out and pass away, but the real person living inside the house will live forever. Ecclesiastes 12:7 says the body returns to the ground from which it came and "the spirit returns to God who gave it." This means spirituality is not something that is happening outside of me or around me, but *within* me. Being spiritual has to do with what is going on between God and me, not about outward religious acts. Think about this scripture: "God . . . works in you to will and to act according to his good purpose" (Phil. 2:13). God is at work where? *In you!*

The psalmist David frequently spoke of God as "*my* God." "The Lord is *my* shepherd," he said (Ps. 23:1). This is one of the features that make his psalms so meaningful. I think this is why God called him "a man after my own heart" (Acts 13:22). David's personal closeness to God—his pursuit of God and the fact that he walked with God and conversed with God throughout the common day—made him a man after God's heart.

"The Lord . . . is at my right hand, I will not be shaken," he wrote (Ps. 16:8). "Though I walk through the valley of the shadow of death, I will fear no evil, for you are with me" (23:4). David had the awareness that God was not a million miles away across the galaxy seated on His throne, but that God was standing next to him. He walked with God. God filled his thoughts. "I think of you through the watches of the night," he wrote (63:6). And he knew that God thought about him: "How precious to me are your thoughts, O God! How vast is the sum of them! Were I to count them, they would outnumber the grains of sand. When I awake, I am still with you" (139:17-18).

Abraham was called "God's friend" (James 2:23). Moses spoke with God "face to face, as a man speaks with his friend" (Ex. 33:11). Jesus wants us to have that closeness with Him, so He said: "I no longer call you servants. . . . I have called you friends" (John 15:15).

True spirituality means a real relationship with God. Spirituality is simple; religion is complex. So, there is a big difference between being spiritual and being religious. The simpler my relationship with God, the more meaningful it is. I think that's why people who are in strict religious environments feel so empty. They are full of traditions, doctrines, and regulations but not full of joy. They are filled with their own theological ideas but feel isolated from God. Adam *walked* with God, but all they do is *work* for their religion. There is a big difference between *walking* and *working*. Which word best describes your relationship with God? Stop doing so much religious work and start walking with God.

Here is a true story about keeping it simple. A Sunday school teacher said to her kids, "If I sold my house and my car, had a big garage sale and gave all my money to the church, would I get into heaven?"

"No!" the children all replied.

"If I cleaned the church every day, mowed the grass, and kept everything neat and tidy, would I get into heaven?"

Again, the answer came, "No!"

"Well," she said, "then how can I get to heaven? What do I have to do first?"

One boy shouted, "You gotta be dead!"

SIT DOWN AND LISTEN UP

There is a story in Jesus' life that teaches how to have a re-lationship with the Lord instead of being bogged down in religion. Luke tells the story this way:

> As Jesus and his disciples were on their way, he came to a village where a woman named Martha opened her home to him. She had a sister called Mary, who sat at the Lord's feet listening to what he said. But Martha was distracted by all the preparations that had to be made. She came to him and asked, "Lord, don't you care that my sister has left me to do the work by myself? Tell her to help me!"
>
> "Martha, Martha," the Lord answered, "you are worried and up-set about many things, but only one thing is needed. Mary has chosen what is better, and it will not be taken away from her" (10:38-42).

Notice that Martha is the one who invites Jesus to their home. She is very hospitable. But while she is fixing dinner, her sister Mary sits at the Lord's feet listening to what He says. That state-ment defines true spirituality.

Mary is not talking; she is listening. She is not doing something; she is listening. She is so happy that Jesus is at their home and she tunes in to every word He is saying. She is getting the most out of this rare and special moment.

Here is the point of contrast: but Martha is *distracted* by all the preparations that have to be made. She comes to Jesus in frustration and demands, "Lord, don't You care that my sister has left me to do the work by myself? Tell her to help me!" What's really going on here? Martha is the one who invited Jesus to their home, but she's not spending one minute with Him. He's in the house but she's in the kitchen doing her own thing. What's the point of inviting Jesus to your house and ignoring Him?

Martha was distracted by a lot of things. Jesus was in her house, but she wasn't experiencing His presence. It's the same with us. God is right here, but we're distracted by so many things that we're not tuned in to Him. We fail to experience His presence. We are not "practicing the presence of the Lord" as Andrew Murray called it.

Martha focused on herself. "Tell her to help *me*." There was nothing wrong with her getting dinner ready. Somebody has to fix the meal. Thank God for the Marthas of the world who fix the meals and keep the house in perfect order. That is not the point of this story. Mary is not a better person than Martha. That is what religious people conclude from this story. They are always thinking about who is better than somebody else. They haven't figured out yet that everybody is a sinner saved by grace, including them. Mary shows us the way of real spirituality—sitting at Jesus' feet.

"Martha," Jesus replied, "you are worried and upset about many things." The phrase "many things" speaks to the complexities of life. Our schedules, jobs, hobbies, commitments, emergencies, and responsibilities all add up to "many things." In contrast to "many things," Jesus said, "only one thing is needed." Spirituality is simple; religion is complicated. Mary had chosen what is better, and Jesus said it would not be taken away from her. She chose to experience His presence instead of being distracted by the pressures of life. It was a rare and special privilege to have Jesus in their home, and Mary was not going to miss it.

We miss out on the presence of God so often because we too are distracted, worried, and upset by many things. But when Jesus comes over, it is time to cancel dinner plans and order in pizza!

Jesus gives us one thing to do in order to have eternal life—believe in Him. "The one who believes [in Me] has eternal life" (John 6:47). However, religious people will give you a whole list of things to do—rules to keep and doctrines to believe. Jesus opens the doors of heaven to us and religious people slam it with their rules and doctrines. Jesus' way is easy; theirs is hard.

MEASURING SPIRITUALITY

While speaking at a minister's conference, a pastor asked me, "How can we measure spirituality?" He said that in his tradition, people measured spirituality by how demonstrative and emotional they acted in a worship service. He wanted to teach his congregation what true spirituality is. I gave him Jesus' answer, saying *spirituality* means two things: "Love the Lord your God with all your heart" and "love your neighbor as yourself" (Matt. 22:37-39). The rest of Scripture agrees that these two commands sum up true spirituality. It is measured by our relationships with God and others, plain and simple.

One day some religious leaders got into a debate with Jesus about the resurrection of the dead. His wisdom prevailed over their tradition. "Hearing that Jesus had silenced the Sadducees, the Pharisees got together" (v. 34). Jesus had answered the Sadducees in such a way that He silenced them. That's exactly what you and I need to do with the religious baggage that's been put in our heads. Maybe people meant well, but a lot of the ideas we have about God, the Christian faith, the Bible, and life are incorrect and we need to silence them. Silence the voices of tradition in your head so you can hear the truth.

Not all the Sadducees were bad people with the wrong intent toward Jesus. But they did err by following their traditions, rules, and theological perspectives instead of Scripture, so Jesus silenced them.

Then one of the teachers of the law asked Him, "Teacher, which is the greatest commandment in the Law?" (v. 36). There are 613 Old Testament laws according to Judaism, so He had a lot of laws from which to choose. Jesus answered him with one chief word—*love*. Love is about relationships. Love is something people share. True spirituality is always relational.

First, Jesus said, "Love the Lord your God." He did not say to love God in some abstract sense as though God were distant and detached from us, but love Him because He is here with us. He did not say love the idea of God or love your religion; rather, love the Lord *your God* with all your heart, soul, and strength. He was quoting Deuteronomy 6:4, so He was not making up a new religion. That is a misconception some people have about Jesus.

He was teaching the Old Testament to people who thought of themselves as experts in the Law. But they had added so much tradition to Scripture that they forgot the greatest commandment. You and I can get so caught up in our religious views that we forget what real spirituality is, just like they did.

FIRST THINGS FIRST

Jesus said the commandment to love the Lord your God is the *first* and *greatest* commandment (Matt. 22:38). What did He mean by "first" since it was not the first commandment God gave in the Old Testament? God told Adam not to eat from the Tree of Knowledge of Good and Evil. So that was the first commandment. Jesus means loving God is first in priority; it is the most important commandment. To love the Lord our God is the most important principle of life and our highest priority. This is the principle that puts us on the right path. Miss this one and we will miss everything else.

If you don't get a spirituality of love, you will end up with a spirituality of law. God loves you with an amazing love. "God so loved the world that he gave his one and only Son that whoever believes in him shall not perish but have eternal life." Jesus said that in John 3:16. That is not some slogan people created to put on a billboard or wear on a T-shirt. No, that was Jesus' summation of who God is and how deeply God cares about us. God *so* loved.

The command to love the Lord is the natural response we have to God when we discover that He loves us! We don't obey the command because we are trying to earn His love but because He loves us. The Scripture says, "We love because he first loved us" (1 John 4:19). *Love* is the first and most important principle of life and defines what it means to "be spiritual."

When I say, "I'm spiritual, not religious," it means the driving force of my life and the motivation of my actions is my love for God and my love for others because He first loved me so much that He gave His only Son for my salvation.

Spirituality is not something you do on Sunday or on the Sabbath day. It is not some habitual prayers or a Bible study you do at a set time each day where you work God into your schedule. That is how religious people think. That makes about as much sense as me saying, "I'll work my wife into my schedule." I can tell you that wouldn't go over very well with her. I married her because I love her and wanted to be with her. I talk to her all the time; she's my life, not an appointment I put on my schedule. But that is how some people think about God, and that is the trap of religion. You don't schedule spirituality any more than you schedule love. A relationship is constant. I have always avoided the phrase "devotional time" with God and chose, instead, to be devoted to Jesus. My time with Jesus is 24/7. He is always with me. As David said, "The Lord . . . is at my right hand, I will not be shaken" (Ps. 16:8).

TRAVELING TOGETHER

Jesus goes on to say the second commandment is like the first: "Love your neighbor as yourself" (Matt. 22:39). That's from Leviticus 19:18. He connects these two great commandments as one. You cannot detach these two. They travel together, moving in tandem. Being *spiritual* means loving God because He loves us so much, and then we share that love with others.

The apostle Paul learned this lesson the hard way. He was a Pharisee, a man who thought of spirituality as keeping the Law—following the rules and keeping the customs of his religion. Yet, he writes, "Let no debt remain outstanding, except the continuing debt to love one another" (Rom. 13:8). The Bible says we can have debts only if we can pay them. Then, in the same verse, Paul says, "He who loves his fellowman has fulfilled the law." That is amazing—if you truly love your neighbor, you have fulfilled the law of God.

All the Ten Commandments "are summed up in this one rule: 'Love your neighbor as yourself.' Love does no harm to its neighbor. Therefore love is the fulfillment of the law" (vv. 9-10). The next time someone says you've got to love but you also have to keep all these other rules they give you, don't! If we truly love God, then we won't violate His commandments—do not covet, do not commit adultery, do not steal, do not bear false witness against your neighbor, and so on.

The minister who asked me that question about how to measure spirituality was dealing with this same issue. He said his congregation gauged the work of God by how exuberant people were in their worship service. Then he asked, "Are there any other ways to measure spirituality?" I am not sure that how people act in a public worship service is a measure of anything at all. But there are some real ways of measuring spirituality—having a true relationship with God as opposed to just acting in religious ways or practicing religious traditions.

True spirituality is a personal relationship with God. Jesus summed up all the commandments of God in two: "Love the Lord your God with all your heart . . . soul . . . and strength," and "love your neighbor as yourself." Then He added, "There is no commandment greater than these" (Mark 12:30-31). The rabbis identified 613 commandments in the Old Testament—265 positive and 348 negative—yet Jesus said, "All the Law and Prophets hang on these two commandments" (Matt. 22:40).

A SINGLE COMMAND

The entire law is summed up in a single command: 'Love your neighbor as yourself'" (Gal. 5:14). Paul can say this because "love does no harm to its neighbor. Therefore love is the fulfillment of the law" (Rom. 13:10). Mark those words—*love does no harm*. Misguided religion can harm. Legalism and judgmental attitudes do harm. Traditions and self-righteousness do cause harm. But love does no harm.

The key here is *love, not law*. Jesus fundamentally defined *spirituality* in terms of relationships. The purest way you measure spirituality is by your personal communion with God and how you treat other people. The more conversational you are with the Lord, the more you can recognize and experience the immediate presence of the Lord with you. The more you speak to Him as your Father, to Jesus as your Lord and listen to Him, the more you are going to experience what a real relationship with God means.

We don't need to be in the business of measuring other people's spirituality. People need to resign from their position as judge. "Examine yourselves," Paul says (2 Cor. 13:5). We can measure our own spirituality by how we treat others. If I don't have love I am only "a resounding gong or a clanging cymbal"—just making noise (1 Cor. 13:1)!

The apostle James calls loving "your neighbor as yourself . . . the royal law found in Scripture" (2:8). John makes the case: "If anyone has material possessions and sees his brother in need but has no pity on him, how can the love of God be in him? . . . Let us not love with words or tongue but with actions and in truth. This then is how we know we belong to the truth" (1 John 3:17-19).

The only time the word *religion* appears in the Bible is in James 1:26-27: "If anyone considers himself religious and yet does not keep a tight rein on his tongue, he deceives himself and his religion is worthless. Religion that God our Father accepts as pure and faultless is this: to look after orphans and widows in their distress and to keep oneself from being polluted by the world." If you consider yourself religious, you will keep a tight rein on your tongue. That's interesting! That shows us all how far from real spiritual maturity we are because we all have a struggle keeping a tight rein on our words. Then he says it boils down to caring for orphans and widows in their distress. That's real religion, real spirituality—caring for people who are less fortunate than we are—and then he adds we ought to keep our personal lives from being contaminated by the world.

True spirituality is about relationships, not religious rituals. Loving God with all my heart and loving you as I love myself is the simplest and purest way to be spiritual, not religious. Mother Theresa said it well in "Garment of Love":

Love has a hem to her garment
that reaches the very dust.

It sweeps the streets and lanes,
and because it can, it must.

A seminary student stayed up all night studying for his final exam. His grades were not very good in this particular course, so he really needed to do well on this exam. As he ran across the campus and started up the stairs, he passed a beggar sitting on the stairs outside the building. As he reached the top of stairs, he thought about the beggar. *Should I go back and help him or go take the exam?* he asked himself. If he helped the beggar he would miss the exam and fail the course. But how could he pass the man by? He decided to help the man. Going back down the stairs, he talked with the man and took him to breakfast. He spent the morning getting him help and returned to the dorm. He knew he had failed the course. When he returned for the final class, the professor prepared to distribute the graded exams. Before doing so, he said to the class, "Only one student made an *A* on this exam." And he called out this student.

The student said, "How can I make an *A*? I didn't even take the exam."

The teacher replied, "I planted the beggar by the stairs to see if you really learned what I have taught you about ministry. The beggar was the exam."

STAYING ON TRACK

Three times in his letter to the Colossians, Paul says, "Don't let anyone." Specifically, there are three things you should never allow in your life.

First, "See to it that no one takes you captive through hollow and deceptive philosophy, which depends on human tradition and the basic principles of this world rather than on Christ" (2:8). Don't let people influence you with spiritual teachings that take you away from Jesus. Guard your life.

Second, "Do not let anyone judge you" (v. 16). Jesus told us not to judge others, and here we read we are not to let anyone judge us! I don't know about you, but I find that very liberating. Don't let people judge you by their religious ideas or their personal views. He says don't let people judge you "by what you eat or drink, or with regard to a religious festival, a New Moon celebration or a Sabbath day." Now religious festivals were (and are) an important part of Israel, just as Christians honor certain seasons of the year like Christmas, Easter, and Sunday as the day of our Lord's resurrection. But the point of these worship experiences is to bring people closer to God, not just to go through religious activities. He says don't let other people judge you by what you eat or drink or by your particular approach to certain holy days.

Then he says something very important: "These are a shadow of the things that were to come; the reality, however, is found in Christ" (v. 17). The Old Testament festivals like Passover and

Pentecost, and even the Sabbath Day, all pointed to Jesus. They were all designed to teach us something about the person and ministry of Jesus. They were the shadow; Jesus is the reality. Religion tends to focus on the shadow and the image rather than the reality. So don't let people judge you. God will ultimately judge our lives, and only He has the authority to do so.

Third, Paul says, "Do not let anyone who delights in false humility and the worship of angels disqualify you for the prize" (v. 18). He talks about mystical spirituality. Some people have a bent toward the weirdest things when it comes to spirituality. They emphasize visions, dreams, and their own ideas which they cannot distinguish from the voice of God. God does give us dreams and visions, but these people are obsessed with them. Everything is a heavenly vision to them; everything is a word from God. They are extremists. Paul says they go into great detail about what they have seen or what they claim to have seen. They think they are spiritual, but the truth is, "[their] unspiritual mind puffs [them] up with idle notions."

Paul had true visions, so he was not opposed to a vision as long as it came from God. He even met Jesus face-to-face in a vision. He writes in the Galatians letter that when he went into the desert of Arabia to prepare for his ministry, Jesus appeared to him. But he doesn't write about the details of that visitation from the Lord nor boast about it, because he knew it was personal and he did not need to make a public show trying to convince others how spiritual he was. Paul did not want people to focus on him but, rather, on Jesus.

He was taken into heaven in a vision. He says he was "caught up to the third heaven . . . to paradise" (2 Cor. 12:2-4). The Jewish concept of "heaven" involves three levels. The *first heaven* is the atmosphere around the earth. The *second heaven* is the spiritual realm of angels and demons. The *third heaven* is paradise, the throne of God. He says when he was taken into the *third heaven*, he saw things too glorious for words. He didn't write a book about everything he saw in heaven; he kept it to himself.

This is one distinguishing mark between true spirituality and false spirituality. False spirituality goes into great detail about what claims to have been seen. It grandstands and draws attention so other people will think we are so high and mighty. Even Mary, the mother of Jesus, "treasured all these things in her heart" when the angel appeared to her telling her she would bring the Messiah to the world (Luke 2:51). She didn't tell everybody about her experience and try to draw attention to herself. Such people exaggerate their experiences to draw attention to themselves. Paul concludes that the reason they act like this is because "they have lost connection" with Jesus (Col. 2:19). When we lose connection with Jesus, we get carried away by false spirituality and superficial religion. So, stay connected to Him!

THE REAL THING

Jesus said unless we are born again we cannot see, or enter, the kingdom of God. When a baby is born, that is just the beginning of life's journey. We expect a baby to grow and develop, go to school and learn, and develop life skills. Babies are born to grow and eventually to become independent. Similarly, being a Christian is a process of becoming all that God created us to be. God saved us with the purpose of "conforming us to the image of his Son" (see Rom. 8:29). If we are in Christ, we are "a new creation"—a new starting point where old things pass away and everything becomes new (2 Cor. 5:17). So, being *spiritual* means we are always in a state of change and growing to become more like Jesus.

Contrarily, religion is cosmetic. Icons are so important in religion because it depends on image, not reality; style, not substance. Religion is like a Christmas tree. Trees are alive, growing and changing. But when you cut one down and put it in the house, it starts dying.

From outward appearances, it looks like it is dynamic, growing, fully alive—but it isn't. Every moment of the day it is dying while its base sits in water. When Christmas is over and you take the tree down, it falls to pieces, leaving pine needles all over the house as you drag it to the road. That is what religion is like—ornamental, but not alive.

THINGS AREN'T ALWAYS HOW THEY APPEAR

A minister gave a children's message on the symbols of the church and the religious garments he wore. He asked the kids, "Why do you think I wear this collar?"

One boy replied, "Because it kills fleas and ticks for up to five months."

That is what some of the religious leaders were like in Jesus' day. They dressed, acted, and prayed in ways that appeared to people as very religious and righteous. They had a "cosmetic religion"; they put a great deal of emphasis on how things looked. But Jesus said, "Unless your righteousness surpasses that of the scribes and Pharisees, you will not enter the kingdom of heaven" (Matt. 5:20 NASB). Why? Because theirs was just an ornamental righteousness, and there was nothing righteous about their character. They emphasized how things looked, what kind of people they socialized with, how many times a day they prayed, and whether or not they kept all their rules. Jesus said to them, "Isaiah was right when he prophesied about you: 'These people worship me with their lips, but their hearts are far from me. They worship me in vain; their teachings are but rules taught by men'" (15:7-9). Later He told them, "You are like whitewashed tombs, which look beautiful on the outside but on the inside are full of dead men's bones and everything unclean" (23:27).

The difference between *religion* and *spirituality* is whether we are really alive, not just wearing the ornaments of religion. Are we growing in grace, developing in character, reflecting the image of Jesus, loving others as God loves us, and walking with God? Or are we more like a Christmas tree with religious decoration but no relationship with God?

We can wear a cross for jewelry but not believe Jesus died for our sins. We can own a Bible but not believe it is the Word of God.

We can attend a religious gathering but not follow Jesus as Lord of our life. We can be a member of a religious organization but not be born again.

Spirituality is like the four seasons of the year. Things blossom at certain times in the Christian life and sometimes they die. Sometimes they are fruitful and sometimes they are barren. Sometimes you are ascending, sometimes you are at a plateau, and sometimes you even fall. That is what the real Christian life looks like. It has ups and downs, plateaus, peaks, and valleys. But in it all, God's Spirit is working in our lives. However, being a Christian does not mean we put on ornaments like a Christmas tree and pretend to be alive. It means we are alive to God and we are growing and changing, not simply pretending to be something we're not.

That's our problem! It is our tendency to judge everything by what we see. We make assessments and assumptions based on the limited view of what we see, and often we draw the wrong conclusions about things and about people. We don't discern what's really going on beneath the surface. Religion is about the outward appearance, while spirituality is about the condition of our souls.

WHAT GOES IN MUST COME OUT

Buddha claimed to receive personal spiritual enlightenment but abandoned his family in the process. We, too, can get so preoccupied with personal enlightenment that we find we are too focused on ourselves. Jesus taught that we find our-selves when we lose ourselves in a life of service. In other words, you lose to win. He taught that the Final Judgment has more to do with outreach than in-reach: "I was hungry and you gave Me food; . . . I was naked and you clothed Me; . . . I was in prison and you came to Me. . . . Inasmuch as you did it to one of the least of these My brethren, you did it to Me" (Matt. 25:35-36, 40 NKJV). The progress of our spiritual life is directly related to how we give ourselves away.

One evening a little girl surprised her family at family prayer time. After she finished praying for her family and herself, she added, "And now, God, what can I do for You?" That's a good prayer to pray.

Israel has two main bodies of water—the Sea of Galilee in the north and the Dead Sea in the south. Three streams of water flow from the mountains in the north to form the fountainhead of the Jordan River. The river flows into the Sea of Galilee and exits the sea on the south, where it continues the length of Israel until finally pouring into the Dead Sea. The Dead Sea has no outlet, so the river stops at that point.

Since the Sea of Galilee has an inlet and outlet, its waters are alive with fish and its banks have vegetation. But the Dead Sea only has an inlet with no outlet. The water is 33 percent mineral content that has built up over the years. There are no fish in its waters and nothing can grow on its shores. The water has such buoyancy that when someone jumps in, he or she immediately rises to the surface. As a kid going to summer camps, I was a terrible swimmer. I sank like a rock. I could not even float on my back—when I tried it, I sank. But all that changed the day I went to the Dead Sea. You can't do anything but float. All you have to do is lie there and you will float like a canoe.

The rabbis always used these two seas to describe two kinds of people. Some are like the Sea of Galilee; they receive the blessings of God and share them with others. They have an inlet and an outlet. But others are like the Dead Sea; they take in, but they never give out. They receive, but they don't give. Am I like the Sea of Galilee, receiving from God and sharing His grace with others? Or am I like the Dead Sea, taking in the blessings but keeping them all to myself? The growth and vitality to life comes in giving ourselves away in service to others. True spirituality is outward, not just inward.

Is your life like a pond or like a river? Jesus said when the Holy Spirit comes to live within us, "from [your] innermost being will flow rivers of living water" (John 7:38 NASB). A pond sits stagnant, but a river is moving and flowing. Do you know the one statement of Jesus that appears more than any other in the Gospels? It is Matthew 16:25: "Whoever wants to save his life will lose it, but whoever loses his life for me [and the gospel] will find it" (see also Mark 8:35; Luke 9:24). When we lose our time, our money, and our ambition and become givers, we begin to understand what it means to be "spiritual."

We have to let the river of God's love flow out of our hearts to others. The self-serving, self-centered life is like the Dead Sea: lifeless, unproductive, and stagnant. The life that is centered on loving and serving others is one of joy, power, and purpose. Real success is measured by how much we give, not by how much we get.

Spirituality is about becoming a better person—a person who treats others the way God relates to them. In the Information Age people want knowledge. We consume information via the Internet. Information is at our fingertips with Google and Wikipedia. We do the same spiritually, wanting to get all the information about God we can. We think we can study our way to heaven. But that is only a small part of spiritual life. Bible study is not nearly as important as Bible living! "Do not merely listen to the word, and so deceive yourselves. Do what it says" (James 1:22).

When the Bible speaks of "knowing God," it means knowing Him in the sense that you know a friend, your parents, or your husband or wife. It is a relational term, not an academic one. It is learning to know Jesus so that I can live like Him. As John writes, "In this world we are like him" (1 John 4:17). It's not learning for the sake of learning. You can study theology all you want, but if you don't have a meaningful relationship with God, what does it matter? That's like studying music theory but being unable to play an instrument and make music. Musicians study music to learn to make music; learning is a pathway to performance. Reading the Bible is not an end in itself; it is a pathway to life. David said, "Your word is a lamp to my feet and a light for my path" (Ps. 119:105).

THE FRIEND OF SINNERS

The Pharisees were separatists. The name *Pharisee* means "pious one" or "separated one." They stayed away from people whom they judged to be sinners. But Jesus met people at their point of need. He went where people were and He was criticized for it. Some labeled Him "a friend of . . . sinners" (Matt. 11:19).

Aren't we called to live a separated life? Absolutely! But to live a separated life simply means we are to avoid sin. It doesn't mean we are to separate from people who need the love of God. It doesn't mean to act like we are better than other people or too good to associate with them. We cannot abandon people or judge them with a condescending attitude. Jesus was out there, on the streets, in houses, in the public arena with common people in the struggles of life, redeeming them from sin and suffering. We are not supposed to isolate ourselves but to infiltrate the dark places of this world with the light of Christ as we "shine like stars in the universe" (Phil. 2:14).

How do we expect to be the light of the world if we don't live in the world? We must meet people, build relationships, and talk with people about the love of God. We must spend time with people who aren't like us and who don't share our faith so we can share the hope we have in Jesus Christ. If all we do is hang out with people who share our faith and values, how are we ever going to introduce others to Jesus? How exactly are we supposed to be the salt of the earth and the light of the world if our narrow definition of spirituality is going to Christian gatherings only? Jesus prayed for us to be in the world but not of it: "My prayer is not that you take them out of the world but that you protect them from the evil one" (John 17:15).

I think the title "friend of sinners" was the greatest title Jesus was ever given. Some religious leaders called Him that as a criticism, but I think it was a great compliment. This title shows His compassion for people regardless of their problems, politics, or perspectives. The religionists called Him "a friend of sinners" because He didn't isolate Himself from people like they did. Jesus related to people on their level. You may say, "I can't go to that place or be around those people because I'm too spiritual." That's not being spiritual; that's being religious in a bad way.

True spirituality goes into the world to help people where they are. God so loved the world. Jesus left heaven to live with us. He moved into our neighborhood—"the Word became flesh and made his dwelling among us" (John 1:14). Since Jesus, the living Word of God, lived with us, then we need to take His Word that is in our hearts into the world as a bright light of hope dispelling the darkness. We too can earn the title "friend of sinners" if we will help people at their point of need.

OUT OF THE SALTSHAKER

Jesus' command to us was not "Therefore, come," but "Therefore, go." Getting together for worship is great and important in our spiritual life. Christianity is community. We are the family of God, and families get together. But our work is in the world.

"Life is a place of service," Leo Tolstoy said. "Joy can be real only if people look upon their life as a service and have a definite objective in life outside themselves and their personal happiness."

We still have the Mount of Transfiguration problem that occurred when Moses and Elijah appeared with Jesus (Matt. 17:1-5). Jesus had taken Peter, James, and John with Him on the mountain for a time of prayer, when they were overwhelmed by this supernatural visitation. Then the voice of God spoke and they were terrified. Peter said, "Let's build three tabernacles and stay here!" It was so incredible that they wanted to stay in that atmosphere of the divine presence. But Jesus said, "Let's go back down the mountain to care for the people." We too want to stay at a place of spiritual ecstasy and joy, but we need to get back to the business of living. Our place is the human realm, not the divine.

A spiritual revival seems to be little more these days than a gathering of people marked by enthusiasm, entertainment, and emotion. There is nothing wrong with that as long as it propels us to take positive action with our faith. The Old Testament prophets and Jesus called for social justice as the result of true revival. Gathering for worship is great, but it is the scattering of God's people where the ministry happens. Jesus said, "The field is the world" (Matt. 13:38). Our work takes place in the world; our worship takes place in the church. We are to be the "salt of the earth" and "the light of the world" (5:13-14).

The Civil Rights Movement began in the U.S. as a Christian movement under the leadership of Martin Luther King and others who were ministers, leaders, and educators. Dr. King and other leaders met in cities with people for prayer services, preaching, and marching in the streets until justice came. They pointed out that our nation's laws were discriminatory. They often quoted Scripture to call the nation to change its ways. They were willing to march on the streets and even on the U.S. Capitol in peaceful demonstrations to deliver the message of Jesus to "love thy neighbor as thyself." The Civil Rights Movement was a Christian revival. A *revival* is when people start treating each other like God commands and life starts changing in the streets. Dr. King took the gospel out of the saltshaker and sprinkled it on the world and things changed for the better.

We are to be a prophetic voice of truth and hope to the nation. There is a difference between Christians speaking out on political or economic issues and speaking out prophetically against injustice and sin. The church must call the nation to turn to God in repentance, humility, and faith. Anything that robs people of their independence and freedom needs to be confronted as wrong in the eyes of God, for "where the Spirit of the Lord is, there is freedom" (2 Cor. 3:17).

The first word of the Great Commission (the only commission Jesus gave) is *go*. The commission is not to stay but to go. Instead of merely going to church, we ought to *be* the church. Jesus told His disciples, "Go [into all the world] and make disciples of all nations" (Matt. 28:19; see also Mark 16:15). Then the Holy Spirit came on the Day of Pentecost and filled them with power. Peter proclaimed the good news of eternal life in Jesus, and three thousand people believed in Christ and were baptized that day! They were off to such a great start! Then the movement grew to five thousand believers in Jerusalem. The problem was they just stayed in Jerusalem when the commission was to *go*.

SCATTERING THE GATHERED

There is a pivotal statement about the timeline of the early church in the Book of Acts: "On that day a great persecution broke out against the church at Jerusalem, and all except the apostles were scattered" (8:1). This happened after an angry religious mob stoned Stephen in the streets of Jerusalem for preaching salvation in Jesus. While he was dying, he prayed, "Lord, do not hold this sin against them" (7:60). The next statement, in chapter 8, is "A great persecution broke out . . . and all except the apostles were scattered."

The word *scattered* is important. As tragic as the persecution was, it did scatter the believers into the world. Jesus calls us "the salt of the earth," but salt in the saltshakers is useless. Sometimes God needs to shake us out of our comfort zone to get back to our mission of being in the world.

James calls believers those who have been "scattered abroad" (James 1:1 NKJV). So does Peter, who writes his first letter "to God's elect, strangers in the world, scattered throughout" (1 Peter

1:1). Peter learned the lesson the hard way. He thought his mission was only to his own people, the Jews. God gave him a vision of all kinds of non-kosher foods and told him to eat the meal (Acts 10:9-16). Peter said, "I can't eat that because it's unclean." God told Peter, "Don't call unclean what I have made clean." The vision was not about food, but about people. Peter had some ethnic pride that needed to be broken.

So God sent him to the house of a Roman centurion who also worshiped God but did not know about Jesus. Peter went with a few others who had the same bigotry. When he entered the home of Cornelius, he said, "You are well aware that it is against our law for a Jew to associate with a Gentile or visit him. But God has shown me that I should not call any man impure or unclean" (v. 28). He went on to say, "I now realize how true it is that God does not show favoritism but accepts men from every nation who fear him and do what is right" (vv. 34-35). He then preached to them about Jesus Christ, and everyone believed and was baptized (see vv. 36-48).

This is an amazing yet perplexing story. First, Jewish law does not forbid Jews to associate with Gentiles (anyone non-Jewish). No such law is in the Old Testament. This is another one of those legalistic rules taught by the Pharisees. Second, Jesus constantly associated with Gentiles, and Peter spent four years with Jesus. How did he miss that? This shows that even though we are Christians, we can be seriously lacking in certain areas of grace and character. Jesus constantly taught His disciples that God so loved the world (that means everyone) that He gave His only Son.

Jesus taught them to love everyone as He loved them. Jesus told them to go to all "nations," which means all people groups. So how could Peter have the audacity to say, "God has shown me" (v. 28)? God had been showing him for the last four years of his life as he walked with Jesus, but I guess he missed the critical lesson—to love everyone as God has loved us. Well, it is better late than never. From that day on, Peter became a man who cared about the whole world and wanted them to know about Jesus Christ, not just people who were like him. He was finally out of the saltshaker!

Some people put a big emphasis on fasting as though fasting for extended periods is going to change everything in the world. But fasting doesn't change the world; it changes you by making you more sensitive to God's will, less focused on yourself, and more concerned for others. God asks, "Is this the kind of fast I have chosen, only a day for a man to humble himself? . . . Is that what you call a fast?" (Isa. 58:5). He goes on, "Is not this the kind of fasting I have chosen: to loose the chains of injustice and untie the cords of the yoke . . . to share your food with the hungry and to provide the poor wanderer with shelter?" (vv. 6-7). That sounds more like a fast from selfishness than it does from food.

There is nothing magical or mystical about fasting. Fasting is not for us but rather to get us outside of ourselves and in the world to help relive oppression and suffering. Fasting doesn't help you get your prayers answered. God will do that for you if you ask Him in simple faith. It is rather to help you become the answer to someone else's prayer. Fasting a day makes you hungry so that you do something about people who are starving to death. Fasting is about self-denial, not self-indulgence. Spirituality and self-centeredness never travel together. The first thing Jesus did when He finished His forty-day fast in preparation for His ministry was to preach the "good news to the poor, . . . to proclaim freedom for the prisoners and recovery of sight for the blind, to release the oppressed" (Luke 4:18). Nowhere in the Bible do we read of people fasting for their personal needs to be met, but rather to prepare themselves to minister to others.

GIVE ME LIBERTY

Patrick Henry said, "Give me liberty or give me death." That's a great statement not only for politics but also religion. Here is a big difference between *religion* and *spirituality*: Religion often is bondage, whereas spirituality is freedom. I'm fascinated with this truth: "The letter kills, but the Spirit gives life" (2 Cor. 3:6).

When we live by the letter of the law—laws regarding holy days, diet, and/or other religious customs—spiritual death results. God's law is holy, righteous, and good. But the law does not save us. The law reveals our sin and our need of God's salvation. It also gives us the moral boundaries for life. The Holy Spirit gives life. But when we make spirituality nothing more than keeping rules, spiritual death occurs. What is spiritual death? It is spirituality that is lifeless, joyless, boring, and meaningless.

We must not try to live by "the letter of the law." Instead, we should live by the spirit of the law—the meaning and the intent of the law. The letter of the law seeks to legislate every detail of people's lives, leaving no room for personal freedom. A legalistic person who makes their faith a matter of keeping man-made religious rules and who lives by works-righteousness yet claims to be filled with the Holy Spirit is an oxymoron. True spirituality depends on the Holy Spirit to guide our consciences. Legalism tries to control people by tactics of fear and guilt, but the Spirit of God sets us free.

There are people who have "a form of godliness but denying the power" (2 Tim. 3:5). A man injures his hand and goes to the hospital. He goes through the emergency-room doors and finds himself in a hallway with two doors—one marked "Men" and the other "Women." He goes through the one for men, and finds himself in a hallway facing two more doors: "Over 55" and "Under 55." He goes through the one marked "Under 55" and finds himself facing two other doors—"Injury Above the Belt" and "Injury Under the Belt." He goes through the door marked "Over the Belt" only to find himself facing two more doors—"External Injury" and "Internal Injury." He goes through the door marked "External Injury" and faces two more doors—"Major Injury" and "Minor Injury." He goes through the door marked "Minor Injury" and finds himself back in the parking lot. He gets back in the car and his wife asks, "Did you get any help?"

"No," he replied, "but they are well organized."

Religion is well-organized, structured, and regimented; however, it lacks in real power, passion, and purpose. As Jesus said, religion "strains out a gnat and swallows a camel" (see Matt.

23:24). Religion is obsessed with meaningless details and misses the greater truths of loving God and loving others.

Augustine said, "In essentials, unity; in non-essentials, liberty; in all things, charity."

This may come as a surprise, but it is OK for Christians to have different opinions, views, and convictions. Christians even have different political views! Some people try to legislate everything and live by the letter of the law (their laws of what they decide it means to be Christian), but "the letter kills." The Holy Spirit gives us room for personal expression. "Where the Spirit of the Lord is, there is freedom" (2 Cor. 3:17). It is a universal truth—"the letter kills, but the Spirit gives life" (v. 6). You've got to loosen up and lighten up! That burden of religion and tradition you have been carrying all your life is killing you. Put it down and take up the yoke of Christ, for He said, "You will find rest for your souls. For my yoke is easy and my burden is light" (Matt. 11:29-30).

CHRISTIANS AREN'T CLONES!

Christians aren't clones! You are free to think for yourself, be yourself, and express yourself. Now, we do share complete unity in the essentials of our faith. When we believe in Jesus Christ as Savior and Lord, we become Christians. We accept the Bible as the absolute truth and seek to follow its teachings. We believe in everything Jesus said and did and follow Him as the absolute Lord of our lives. So, there is a standard of faith to which we hold as Christians. However, that does not mean we are all going to have the same views or convictions about every area of life, nor should we. On non-essentials and the issues the Bible does not address, we should pray for the Holy Spirit to give us personal direction. We should also think for ourselves and follow our own conscience in personal matters that are not clearly spelled out in Scripture. Remember, sin is "transgression of the law [of God]," not transgression of someone else's personal views (1 John 3:4 KJV). When religious organizations try to legislate people's lives, they bring spiritual death. Remember, the letter kills.

A pastor gave up the ministry after twenty years to become a funeral director. When asked why he made the change, he said, "Well, I spent about twelve years trying to straighten people out. I never could straighten them out, but now when I straighten people out, they stay straight."

Max Lucado said, "Legalism has no pity on people. Legalism makes my opinion—your burden; makes my opinion—your boundary; makes my opinion—your obligation. Nothing will keep a Christian more immature than trying to keep a long list of rules" (*Up Words*, May 1993). If we are champions of grace we will be the enemy of legalism. Legalism makes you feel like you never measure up. It makes you focus on your own performance rather than resting in the grace of God.

The movie *Playing for Time* portrays the story of Fanla Fenelon, a member of an orchestra of Jewish women who were spared the gas chambers at Auschwitz so long as they played well. The lives of these women were reduced to a single proposition: do well or die. When we make our faith a matter of works, we feel God is watching every detail and our salvation depends on our constant perfection. But God's grace keeps us in spite of the occasional missed notes or dissonant chords of our lives. God is "able to keep you from falling and to present you before his glorious presence without fault and with great joy" (Jude 24).

A MOMENT OF CONFLICT

One of the most conflicted moments of my life came when the movie *The DaVinci Code* was released. Personally, I have no interest in the film as a fictional story raising questions regarding the divinity of Jesus. But, as a Christian and a minister, I wanted to be aware of the story and how it might impact people in terms of their spiritual quest. I was shocked when Barbie and I arrived at the theater and there were believers with big protest signs! I felt very conflicted driving past them to get into a movie they were protesting. I certainly protest the fictional idea that Jesus is someone less than the Son of God, but I wanted to see the movie so I could use the story line in my preaching to refute it and to make the biblical case that Jesus is God's Son.

The moment of conflict was that we were all Christians, but they were protesting the movie and we were watching it. It was also a moment of clarity. I realized again that Christians aren't clones and that we have different views. We just had different personal opinions about watching the movie, and that's O.K.. I would even say it's healthy. One of the frightening marks of a cult is that everyone is brainwashed to think and to act like robots.

Those believers had the freedom to protest the movie and I had the freedom to see the movie.

POLITICS AND FAITH

Politics is another hot topic where people have disagreements. It is a mistake to suggest that if people were Christians they would all have the same political views. I was interviewed by the *New York Times* during a presidential election and asked how I thought the "Christian right" would impact the election. I replied, "What about the Christian left?"

The writer was stunned by my response and asked, "What do you mean?"

I said, "Christians don't all share the same political views. There are Christian politicians on both sides of the aisle in Congress. You don't define what it means to be Christian based on someone's political views. The fact is that the overwhelming majority of Americans are Christians. Christians are not some minority fringe movement. They come in a lot of shapes and sizes with a variety of views on politics. What we do agree on is Jesus!" I went on to suggest that he stop following the rhetoric of the day by using the term "Christian right" and fueling people's prejudices and stereotypes and write an article of real interest.

He replied, "I never thought of that before. I think I will take a different angle on the subject when I write the article."

A man said to me during a close election, "If we could just get all the Christians in this country to vote, we could determine the election."

I replied, "No we couldn't, because half would vote Republican and half would vote Democrat, and whoever didn't would vote Independent . . . and we'd still be in the same mess we're in now." He seemed shocked when I went on to remind him that Christians don't all share the same political views. He naively believed that all Christians either shared his views on everything or, worse, that they *should* share his views on everything.

Keep in mind what it means to be a Christian. It means to personally believe in and follow Jesus Christ as Lord of one's life. It means to deny ourselves, take up our cross, and follow Him daily (Luke 9:23). It doesn't mean you belong to one political party or another. America is a nation of freedom of religion, worship, and conscience. Christians have different views on politics, education, and economics, and that is OK as long as their views don't contradict Scripture. We must always align our views with God's Word. To be truly Christian will shape the way we exercise our religious freedom and where we stand on the issues.

A synagogue was split down the middle on a contentious question—whether to stand or sit during the reading of the *Shema*. Half of the congregation insisted that, in the old days, the congregation always remained seated. The other half was just as convinced that standing was the only appropriate posture for reciting the great words. In despair, the president of the congregation visited the oldest living member and said, "We need to know what is the tradition of our congregation regarding the *Shema* . . . that everyone stands?"

The old man said, "No. I don't remember that we did that."

"O.K.," said the president, "so we all remain seated for the *Shema*."

"No," said the old man. "That wasn't the tradition either."

"Well, which is it?" said the president, somewhat frustrated. "We need to know. Right now, we have half the congregation sitting and yelling at the half that is standing. Half the congregation is standing and screaming at the half that is sitting!"

"Yes," said the old man. "That is our tradition!"

DON'T SWEAT THE DETAILS

Jesus calls for unity among His people. While we are to hold firmly to the foundational truths of faith, we are not to sweat every detail of people's personal views on matters that are not addressed in the Bible. There is plenty of room for our differences as Christians. Paul turns his attention in Romans 14 to how Christians are to live in unity in spite of their differences of opinions and personal convictions. Consider verses 1-3:

> Accept him whose faith is weak, without passing judgment on disputable matters. One man's faith allows him to eat everything, but another man, whose faith is weak, eats only vegetables. The man who eats everything must not look down on him who does

not, and the man who does not eat everything must not condemn the man who does, for God has accepted him.

Don't pass judgment on disputable matters. The word *judge* (Greek, *krino*) means to "criticize" or "decide." So *judgment* has both a positive and a negative application. We don't need to try to settle disputable points of faith and practice. Those areas of life that are not specifically addressed in Scripture are matters of personal conviction. Do not look down on people who have different convictions, for you share the same faith in Christ. The Christian faith rests on the foundation of Christ and Scripture, not on traditionalism. It is broad enough to handle diversity on matters that are not essential to our faith. God has accepted us, and we need to extend the same courtesy and grace to one another.

Paul goes on to ask, "Who are you to judge someone else's servant? To his own master he stands or falls. And he will stand, for the Lord is able to make him stand" (v. 4). We aren't qualified to judge others. Jesus said, "Do not judge" (Matt. 7:1). Paul said he did not even judge himself, much less was subject to the judgment of others (1 Cor. 4:3). The Lord is able to make us all stand as He works in us what is pleasing to Him. Why do we judge others? This is a thought-provoking question each of us must consider. What motivates us to be judgmental? This may be the most common sin among mature Christians—criticizing others.

Henry Saint John wrote: "Should a man not lay his hand upon his mouth before he criticizes his brothers? When we pass swift, uninformed, unloving, and ungenerous judgments, surely we have forgotten that if we speak evil of them, at the same time we speak evil of the Lord whose name they bear."

Jesus Christ alone is Lord and Judge. We will all stand before Christ's judgment seat and give an account of ourselves to God. We are answerable *to* each other but not *for* each other.

Now, for those who argue about which day of the week we should worship God, Paul writes: "One man considers one day more sacred than another; another man considers every day alike. Each one should be fully convinced in his own mind" (Rom. 14:5). We need to think things through so that we are fully convinced in our own minds about worship. Show respect for other people's views on matters that are not specifically addressed in Scripture.

The passage reaches its crescendo with the statement, "Therefore let us stop passing judgment on one another" (v. 13). Christians are free in Christ but are to use our freedom for the good of all. "Do not use your freedom to indulge the sinful nature; rather, serve one another in love" (Gal. 5:13). We should practice our freedom in love to act in the best interest and spiritual welfare of others. This does not mean we are to allow the legalism of others to limit our freedom and to come into bondage to their narrow views. But we are to consider the impact of our behavior on others and to teach those who are weak in their faith the way of liberty.

Finally, "Do not allow what you consider good to be spoken of as evil. For the kingdom of God is not a matter of eating and drinking, but of righteousness, peace and joy in the Holy Spirit. . . . Let us therefore make every effort to do what leads to peace and to mutual edification" (Rom. 14:16-17, 19). What we consider "good" must never become the subject of slanderous talk.

First, those who are free to do something should not flaunt their liberty in a spirit of arrogance. Second, those who are limited in their liberty must refrain from judging those who are free. The kingdom of God is about the larger matters of life. Jesus corrected the Pharisees and teachers of the law for "straining out gnats and swallowing camels" (see Matt. 23:24). Legalists focus on small, non-essential details of religion and miss the big picture of God's work in the world. They suffer from tunnel vision regarding God and life.

Since we have different opinions and convictions, we need to remember the closing lesson of the Romans 14 passage: "So whatever you believe about these things keep between yourself and God. Blessed is the man who does not condemn himself by what he approves" (v. 22). Enjoy your own freedom, but keep it to yourself. Happiness comes from not putting yourself in a religious, legalistic box. It is a sin to violate your own convictions. The blessing comes from not making more laws for yourself than God requires of you to keep. Let others be free to express themselves, think for themselves, and live out their faith as they choose.

VEILS ON OUR FACES

On one occasion some religious leaders brought Jesus a Roman coin and asked if they were supposed to pay taxes. They did it to "trap him" (Matt. 22:15). They wanted to find one small thing in the Roman law where they could criticize. On another occasion they brought to Him a woman who had been caught in adultery and asked Him what to do. Again, they did this to test Him to see if He would violate the law of Moses (John 8:1-6).

In both of these stories, the religionists missed the meaning of the law and looked only at the exact wording to see if they could trap Jesus. Religion focuses on the letter of the law. You've got to cross every "t" and dot every "i." If we live by the letter—by every little rule that everybody demands of us—then we will live in bondage. Do we live by the intent of the law?

Some people try to make the Bible say anything they want it to say. They twist the Scriptures to their own destruction. They don't have a clue what the Bible is about. People justify all kinds of non-Christian ideas in the name of Jesus because they look only at the letter of the law. They find one isolated statement in Scripture that backs up their view, but they miss the spirit of the law, the real meaning of the passage. If they read the entire Bible they would realize how misguided they are. But they isolate a single statement. Remember, "the letter kills, but the Spirit gives life" (2 Cor. 3:6). If you build anything on the letter of the law, it will destroy whatever you are building.

You've got to see the big picture of the nature and will of God in Scripture. Unfortunately, Christians divide themselves over the least significant issues and miss the big picture of unity. Some believers and organizations isolate themselves from other believers, thinking and telling themselves they have all the answers and everyone else is wrong. Jesus came to unify us, but we separate ourselves over the least significant issues of faith.

The term "letter of the law" also refers to writing things down. That's what legalists do; they want to write everything down and make a hard-and-fast rule for all time and for all people. They have no flexibility. But life is meant to be flexible on some points. We should grow and change as a normal part of life. Just because the Ten Commandments were written in stone doesn't mean we are to do the same with all our beliefs. God can put His law in stone because it is absolute. But our personal views on things are not absolute and we need to change them when we realize we were wrong or the generation who raised us was wrong.

We don't have the right in Christ to write laws and rules for people outside the teachings of Scripture and then say if people don't agree then they aren't really Christians. Only you know if you truly believe in and follow Jesus Christ as Lord. The Holy Spirit gives life!

Paul was talking about the old days of Moses when he said, "The letter kills, but the Spirit gives life" (2 Cor. 3:6). Moses was a great man who gave us the Law of God. We need the Law of God because it awakens in us a sense of sin and our need of grace. But the Law doesn't save us; it points us to Jesus.

Moses received the Ten Commandments at Mount Sinai where he was in the presence of God. When he came down from the mountain, his face was radiant and it frightened the people, so they had him put a veil over his face. Over time, the glory diminished because it was not permanent. His normal countenance returned the same way that a good suntan in the summer fades in the winter. Well, the radiance of God's glory on his face faded.

But he kept wearing the veil because he did not want them to know the glory faded. Paul then makes the point that the glory of the Law and days of Moses were not permanent but pointed to the greater glory of Jesus the Messiah.

Now that we are born again we are in the new covenant and we have the permanent glory of the Holy Spirit. In fact, as we grow in our relationship with Jesus, the glory increases! "Where the Spirit of the Lord is, there is freedom. And we, who with unveiled faces all reflect [like mirrors] the Lord's glory, are being transformed into his likeness with ever-increasing glory, which comes from the Lord, who is the Spirit" (vv. 17-18).

DON'T MISS WHAT GOD IS DOING

Paul said of the Israelites, "Their minds were made dull, for to this day the same veil remains when the old covenant is read. It has not been removed, because only in Christ is it taken away. Even to this day when Moses is read, a veil covers their hearts" (2 Cor. 3:14-15). When the Israelites read the Old Testament prophecies of the Messiah, they could not see that Jesus fulfilled them. The people missed the Messiah's appearing even though Jesus fulfilled the Old Testament prophecies.

Many of the religious leaders rejected Jesus because He did not fit into their idea of what the Messiah would be. They had their minds made up and were closed to what God was doing in the world when Jesus came. They had a veil of tradition over their minds that caused them to miss the Messiah's coming. So even though they read the Old Testament, they missed the prophecies of the Messiah fulfilled in Jesus because they had a veil over their minds.

What was true of them is also true of us. We will miss what God is doing in the world if we don't take off our veils of tradition. We have veils on our faces when we read the Bible that keep us from seeing what's in it. People tend to read into the Bible what they want to see. They find Scripture verses to back up their beliefs, even though their beliefs are misguided. We may have been taught what the Bible means, so we read it through the filter of that tradition and don't allow the Bible to speak for itself. But if we took the veil off and read it with new eyes, we would discover exciting truths in God's Word. Instead, we just reinforce our traditions and do not receive a fresh word from God. We need to pray the prayer of David when we read the Bible: "Open my eyes that I may see wonderful things in your law" (Ps. 119:18).

Some people have a Catholic veil over their minds. Others have a fundamentalist veil, an evangelical veil, or a Pentecostal veil. Others have veils of atheism, secularism, new ageism, or universalism. If you are not careful, you will have a religious veil over your mind and you will miss what God desires to show you in His Word.

Religion puts a veil on our faces. The Holy Spirit takes the veil away and "guides [us] into all truth" (John 16:13). If we already knew everything, we would not need the Spirit to continue to guide us into all truth. We need a humble attitude, recognizing we don't know everything and desiring to continue to learn as God shows us wonderful things in His Word.

Plato said, "The unexamined life is not worth living." When we read the Bible we shouldn't say, "I already know what it says." We need to be open for God to show us new things and new applications of His Word. "The Word of God is living and active," and we need to allow it to work on our hearts and minds (Heb. 4:12). The Word of God is given to correct, teach, reprove, and train us (2 Tim. 3:16), but it cannot do that if we already have our prejudices and perspectives poured in concrete. Religion is proud; spirituality is humble. Paul says, "Whenever anyone turns to the Lord, the veil is taken away" (2 Cor. 3:16). Only God can take away the veils that keep us from receiving Christ as our Savior and the religious veils that keep us from understanding His Word. "Where the Spirit of the Lord is, there is freedom" from the veils that keep us from receiving God's Word.

Question the status quo. Think things through for yourself. Don't accept everything you hear. Instead, "test everything. Hold on to the good" (1 Thess. 5:21). Follow the example of the people of Berea, who "examined the Scriptures every day to see if what Paul said was true" (Acts 17:11). If you already have your mind made up about everything, you are going to miss so much of what is in the Bible. But if you have an open mind, God will show you great and mighty things that you do not know.

FATHER OF LIES

The worst veil of all is the veil of deception. "The god of this age has blinded the minds of unbelievers, so that they cannot see the light of the gospel of the glory of Christ" (2 Cor. 4:4). Jesus called the devil "the father of lies" (John 8:44). John the Revelator said the devil "leads the whole world astray" (Rev. 12:9). People are deceived into thinking they can save themselves, or worse, that they don't even need to be saved from their sins. Others are misguided into thinking that all religions lead to God and it doesn't matter what you believe as long as you are sincere. Others are trapped by their own intellect concluding there is no God or, if there is, He is not involved with us. But once we come to know Jesus Christ, those veils of deception are removed.

George Bernard Shaw was renowned as a freethinker and liberal philosopher. In his last writings we read, "The science to which I pinned my faith is bankrupt. Its counsels, that should have established the millennium, led instead, directly to the suicide of Europe. I believed them once. In their name I helped to destroy the faith of millions of worshippers in the temples of a thousand creeds. And now they look at me and witness the great tragedy of an atheist who has lost his faith" (*www.sermonillustrations.com*).

Leo Tolstoy, the noted Russian author, was an atheist. Then he came to know Jesus Christ as his Savior. He wrote: "For 35 years of my life I was, in the proper acceptance of the word, a *nihilist*—not a revolutionary socialist, but a man who believed in nothing. Five years ago my faith came to me. I believed in the doctrine of Jesus, and my whole life underwent a sudden transformation. . . . Life and death ceased to be evil; instead of despair, I tasted joy and happiness that death could not take away" (*My Religion*).

Someone spray-painted graffiti on the wall of a New York subway: "'God is dead.' Signed: Nietzsche." Another person painted over it the words, "'Nietzsche is dead.' Signed: God."

True spirituality brings freedom; religion brings bondage. George Washington said, "It is impossible to rightly govern the world without God and the Bible." Horace Greeley said, "It is impossible to enslave, mentally or socially, a Bible-reading people. The principles of the Bible are the groundwork of human freedom." Jesus said, "You are in error because you do not know the Scriptures or the power of God" (Matt. 22:29).

SCRIPTURE IS SUFFICIENT

We need to live by the supremacy of Scripture. As Paul said, "Do not go beyond what is written" (1 Cor. 4:6). I was at dinner with some leaders of a denomination when one of them remarked, "What we need to do is teach our denominational creed of faith in our churches."

I responded, "What we need to do is teach the Bible." My wife, Barbie, was sitting next to me and gently kicked me under the table so I didn't stir up any controversy.

What various Christian denominations rule about certain matters of faith and life in their conventions and councils is irrelevant if you stop and think about it. I mean, it is certainly irrelevant to God! He has already told us not to add anything to His Word. "Every word of God is flawless. . . . Do not add to his words" (Prov. 30:5-6).

We have the written Word of God, and that is sufficient. The Bible is "God-breathed and is useful for teaching . . . so that the man of God may be thoroughly equipped for every good work" (2 Tim. 3:16-17). The Word of God is all we need to fuel our faith and keep us free from deception.

A minister's son got into his father's sermon notes one Saturday night and got them out of order. As the minister began his sermon on Noah and the ark, he read, "Noah was 120 years old and took a wife who was [turned the page and continued reading] 450 cubits long and 75 cubits high, 35 cubits wide and made of gopher wood pitched within and without with tar."

He paused and then said, "I have never read that before, but I believe the Bible from Genesis to Revelation. That's just clear evidence that we are fearfully and wonderfully made."

Religion prides itself on tradition. Now there are good traditions. Thanksgiving is a great tradition. It is the best cooking in the world. There are some great Christian traditions. But traditions change with time, while the truth remains the same. We never want to confuse tradition with truth. Jesus challenged the traditions of His day, saying, "You nullify the word of God for the sake of your tradition" (Matt. 15:6). When we *nullify* something we make it empty, void, and useless. He asked the Pharisees point-blank, "Why do you break the command of God for the sake of your tradition?" (v. 3). Now that is a strong confrontation worth our consideration. If we aren't careful we will get so used to our religious traditions and so set in our ways that we nullify God's Word and even go to the point of breaking God's commands in order to keep our traditions. So, out with traditions and in with the truth! Don't get religious traditions mixed up with truth, thinking they are the same thing, because they aren't. Tradition often limits us, while the truth liberates us.

Martin Luther was a Reformer who lived in the 1500s. As a young seminary student and preacher, he came to a personal faith in Jesus Christ when he read one passage in Scripture that forever changed his life: "The just shall live by faith" (Rom. 1:17 KJV). He realized for the first time that his eternal salvation was not based on good works, penance, or the absolution of a human priest but on his faith in Jesus Christ. He began to point out where the church of his day had left the authority of Scripture for the sake of their traditions. He was a part of what is called the Great Reformation in Europe.

Martin Luther was a catalyst for the Great Reformation to Germany in the 1500s. He was a young theologian and preacher who confronted the church with its tradition that violated Scripture based on three truths—the authority of Scripture, salvation by grace through faith, and the priesthood of all believers. On October 31, 1521, he nailed his Ninety-five Theses to the door of the Wittenberg Church. He confronted the church of their errors in departing from Scripture and called for a reformation.

Before his religious trial, Luther remained in hiding because of threats on his life. One of his friends, a church leader, appealed to him to recant his challenge of the church's traditions. Luther told him he would not recant anything he had said or written. His friend asked, "When they summon you for trial, where can they find you?"

He replied, "You can find me where I have always been, in the hand of the Almighty."

At his trial, the evidence used against him was all the sermons, articles, and books he had written challenging the traditions of the church and showing how they violated the Scripture. When he was told to retract what he had written and preached, he said, "If you can show me one place in all my works where I published something that is contrary to Scripture, then I will retract my statements challenging the church's traditions." But they could not find one word!

His final words to his accusers were these: "Here I stand, God help me; I cannot do otherwise. Amen." He was excommunicated because he believed the truth of Scripture over the traditions of the church. How contradictory is that? But it shows how we can get in bondage to religious tradition and get fighting mad when the truth challenges those traditions. Luther was excommunicated for heresy when those judging him were the heretics and the hypocrites.

Luther didn't want to get kicked out of the church. He loved the church. He only wanted it to change and to get back to the basics of the Christian faith. He found ninety-five points in the Catholic Church that were wrong! He judged their traditions by the truth and they came up short.

Luther simply showed them where they were out of line with Scripture and they were angry about it. So they excommunicated him, not for the truth, but for their traditions. They didn't want to admit they were wrong. They didn't want any voice telling them that had to change—the same way that traditionalists today will silence any voice of objection, honest questioning, or dissenting view of their traditions. And they certainly don't want anyone to show them in the Bible where they are wrong.

The Reformers wanted Christians to return to the authority of Scripture. They also wanted the people to have the Bible for themselves so they could read it and hear from God. People used to go to church and the priest would read it in Latin. But Gutenberg's printing press changed the world. It enabled the Bible to be translated and printed in common language. When you can read the Bible for yourself, you are free from other people translating it for you or only reading the passages they want you to hear. The Reformers stressed three great truths:

- *Sola Gratia*—salvation by grace alone
- *Sola Fideis*—salvation by faith alone
- *Sola Scriptura*—life by Scripture alone

The Reformers also stressed the fact that Jesus Christ is our only High Priest; He is the only mediator between God and humanity. Christ alone can save us and give us eternal life. Scripture alone can guide us into all truth for life and decisions. Christ alone is my Savior, and Scripture alone is my source of truth. Jesus is the incarnation of truth. He is the way and truth; the person Jesus, God in the flesh; and the Scripture, the Word of God from Genesis to Revelation. He is all I need. Christ and His Word is enough for me.

The Bible is the inspired, inerrant, and infallible Word of God. The truth of Jesus and the truth of Scripture reign over everything else. We do not make the Bible subservient to tradition. That's what the Pharisees did. They taught their rabbinical teachings and traditions as though they were equal to Scripture until the average person did not know the difference between the Scripture and traditions. Unfortunately, we do the same thing today.

Jesus told the Pharisees, "You are in error because you do not know the Scriptures or the power of God" (Matt. 22:29). People today are in error because they don't know the Scriptures or the power of God, and these two go together. It is O.K. to have personal and cultural traditions as long as they aren't unbiblical and don't make you arrogant, causing you to judge other people by them.

Christian spirituality is simple. It is great for us to share our thoughts and opinions and views, but don't ever confuse someone's personal opinion or even the opinion of a whole religious group as the truth of God. The Bible says what it says and we aren't to add one single thing to it. We have complicated and contaminated the purity of the Christian faith over centuries of our own creeds, confessions, and concepts.

One time the great British detective Sherlock Holmes and his very knowledgeable partner, Dr. Watson, went on a camping trip. After a good meal and some quiet time, they lay down for the night, and went to sleep. Some hours later, Holmes awoke and nudged his faithful friend. "Watson, look up at the sky and tell me what you see."

Watson replied, "I see millions and millions of stars."

Sherlock Holmes asked, "What does that tell you?"

Watson pondered for a minute, then said: "Astronomically, it tells me that there are millions of galaxies and potentially billions of planets. Astrologically, I observe that Saturn is in Leo. Horologically, I deduce that the time is approximately a quarter past three. Theologically, I can see that God is omnipotent, and that we are small and insignificant. Meteorologically, I suspect that we will have a beautiful day tomorrow."

Sherlock Holmes replied, "Watson, you idiot. Someone has stolen our tent!"

Let's return to the simple faith of Jesus Christ found in the Gospels and the New Testament. The Word of God is sufficient.

IN THE BEGINNING GOD

Is our spirituality centered on God or on ourselves? Does our faith start with God or with us? We need to live our lives the same way the Bible begins: "In the beginning God." Do we serve God's will or do we want Him to serve our will? Do our prayers have more to do with asking God to give us what we want than seeking His will and purpose in our lives? Do we pray more for our needs or the needs of others? We need to discover the ultimate purpose of life: "Whatever you do, do it all for the glory of God" (1 Cor. 10:31).

When we seek first the kingdom of God and His righteousness, He provides all the other things we need for life (Matt. 6:33). It is when we try to get God to help us build *our* kingdom that we get off track.

True spirituality is God-centered, focused on His will and His glory. Humanism is the new religion of our day. Humanism says man is the measure of all things. But man is not the measure of all things; God is!

We are not an evolutionary accident. We are created in the image of God. In that sense, we have an inherent goodness. But that is not all the story. We are also sinners in need of grace. We are a mixture of good and evil—*good* because we are made in God's image, but *bad* because we have sinned against God. We are in need of His grace to save us from sin so we can be made again in His image.

We are created by God with a higher purpose than serving our own agenda. "In him we live and move and have our being" (Acts 17:28). We live for His glory, "for from him and through him and to him are all things" (Rom. 11:36).

We are too self-focused and self-centered. Too often, we tend to ask, What's in it for me? We evaluate everything by what we are getting out of it. "It's all about me," is the sin nature in a nutshell. I do what I want to do *when* I want to do it. When Jesus saves us from sin, He also saves us from self. He reconnects me with God as my Creator. I am not the source of all things—God is.

The Bible's opening statement is my life mission, "In the beginning God." True spirituality centers my life on God, my Creator. I pray, "Lord, what would You have me do? What is Your counsel? What is Your wisdom?" When God is the center of my life and thoughts instead of me, I start asking a new set of questions. I stop asking what's in it for me and start asking what I can do for others. I stop asking what will make me happy and ask what can I do to bring others joy. I stop asking what do I think about this and ask what does God say about this. We need to all ask the "God question" more than we do the "self question."

The Lord's Prayer (Matt. 6:9-13) never uses a personal pronoun. I find that fascinating. By following this model, we never get to pray for ourselves without, at the same time, praying for God's will and for the needs of others.

- I cannot say *Our* if my religion has no room for others, and their need.
- I cannot say *Father* if I do not demonstrate this relationship in my daily living.
- I cannot say *Who art in heaven* if all my interests and pursuits are in earthly things.
- I cannot say *Hallowed be Thy name* if I, who am called by His name, am not holy.
- I cannot say *Thy kingdom come* if I am unwilling to give up my own sovereignty and accept the righteous reign of God.

- I cannot say *Thy will be done* if I am unwilling or resentful of having it in my own life.
- I cannot say *On earth as it is in heaven* unless I am truly ready to give myself to His service here and now.
- I cannot say *Give us this day our daily bread* without expending honest effort for it, or by ignoring the genuine needs of my fellowmen.
- I cannot say *Forgive us our trespasses, as we forgive those who trespass against us,* if I continue to harbor a grudge against anyone.
- I cannot say *Lead us not into temptation* if I deliberately choose to remain in a situation where I am likely to be tempted.
- I cannot say *Deliver us from evil* if I am not prepared to fight in the spiritual realm with the weapon of prayer.
- I cannot say *Thine is the kingdom* if I do not give the King the disciplined obedience of a loyal subject.
- I cannot say *Thine is the power* if I fear what my neighbors and friends may say or do.
- I cannot say *Thine is the glory* if I am seeking my own glory first.
- I cannot say *Forever* if I am too anxious about each day's affairs.
- I cannot say *Amen* unless I honestly say, "Come what may, this is my prayer" (Author unknown).

Let me end where I began—with the story about the nurse in the hospital who told me, "I'm spiritual, but not religious." I don't know exactly what she meant, but I know what I mean when I say it. I want a true relationship with God and with the Lord

Jesus. I want to be open and honest with Him and tuned in to His presence with me 24/7. I want to love Him because He loves me. I want that love to flow out of me to others.

I don't want to be like a Christmas tree decorated with religious ornaments only appearing to be real and alive. I want to be fully alive and growing in the likeness of Jesus my Lord. I don't want to put on a religious show or pretentious image of spirituality to impress people like the Pharisees of old. I want to be the real thing. I want to be deeply rooted in Christ, growing and developing and changing so that old things are passing away and all things are becoming new.

I don't want to be judged by how I dress, how much money I make, what kind of music I like or my politics, nor do I want to judge others. I want to be accepted as a Christian simply because I believe in Jesus Christ as Lord. I don't want to feel pressured to be like other people or to conform to their narrow view of what they think it means to be spiritual. I want to be accepted and to accept others unconditionally.

I don't want to look at the world around me and say, "What's in it for me?" Rather, I want to say, "Lord, here is my life. I want to honor You and glorify You; I want to be a sacrifice of praise for You."

I don't want to live by the letter of the law that leads to bondage. I want to experience the liberty of the Spirit of God, who will guide me into all truth. I want to know the truth, for the truth shall set me free.

She had it right—*I'm spiritual, but not religious.*

CHRIST ALONE

The Christian faith is focused on the person of Jesus Christ. "Let us fix our eyes on Jesus, the author and perfecter of our faith" (Heb. 12:2). There is no higher authority than Christ himself and the written authority of Scripture for our lives. My allegiance and loyalty is to Jesus Christ, to His people, and to the Scriptures; not to religious or political organizations. Organizations are fine as long as they do the work of Jesus in the world. But when religious organizations start serving their own interests, pursuing their own agenda, and existing only to serve themselves and preserving their traditions, they are useless to the kingdom of God.

Since I was raised in the Presbyterian Church, I found this piece of history fascinating. Two hundred years ago, Barton Stone and several of his associates wrote a document called "The Last Will and Testament of the Springfield Presbytery," in which the denominational organization of which they were members—the Springfield Presbytery of the Presbyterian Church—disbanded so they could be simply Christians.

Every Christian organization or movement gets off track when it gets ingrown and starts serving itself. News commentator Dan Rather had a good way of keeping his professional objective always in mind. He says he often looked at a question he had written on three slips of paper. He kept one in his billfold, one in his pocket, and one on his desk. The probing reminder asked, "Is what you are doing now helping the broadcast?"

The University Christian Movement, with offices in New York City, voted itself out of existence in 1968. On their door, one of the participants posted this sign: "Gone out of business—didn't know what our business was."

We need to read the Gospels more often so we can keep our focus on what Jesus said and did. Luke begins the Book of Acts with these words: "In my former book . . . I wrote about all that Jesus began to do and to teach until the day he was taken up to heaven" (Acts 1:1-2). He wrote about Jesus in what we call the Gospel of Luke. However, the Book of Acts tells us how Jesus continues His ministry in the world through us as He empowers us by the Holy Spirit.

The Holy Spirit lives in us and empowers us to continue to do all that Jesus did and taught. What did Jesus do when He was on this earth? He "went about doing good and healing all who were oppressed by the devil" (10:38 NKJV). Our role as Christians is to continue the ministry of Jesus—nothing more and nothing less. Jesus said we would do greater things than He did because He was going to the Father. True Christians do what Jesus did by showing compassion to everyone and by teaching what Jesus taught, that the kingdom of God is here! You can be born again, be free from the judgment of sin, live eternally in heaven, and live an abundant life here and now!

The Christian community had its birth at Pentecost. There is one body of Christ and we share a common history. The only truth we need is Jesus Christ, and the only authority we need is the Bible. The more we write creeds, codes, and customs, the further we get from Christ. Paul said he resolved to know nothing "except Jesus Christ and him crucified" (1 Cor. 2:2). We need to return to the simple faith given to us by Jesus, who alone is the way, the truth, and the life.

A small rural town was having a centennial celebration. People who had grown up in that town were coming back for a grand homecoming. As a part of the festivities, they had a worship service planned for Sunday morning. Two men were asked to recite Psalm 23 as part of the service. The first speaker was an elderly man who had been a farmer in the community all his life. The other was a young, prestigious lawyer who had grown up in the town but now lived in a metropolitan city. The two men represented the old and the new generations.

The lawyer made his presentation first. His demeanor was captivating. He was a trained speaker and used to making a strong presentation as a defense attorney in a court of law. He delivered a flawless presentation of Psalm 23 from memory, eliciting a resounding applause from the audience.

Then, slowly, the old man made his way to the lectern. With a rough, weatherworn voice, he spoke the timeless words of the psalmist from the depths of his soul. "The Lord is my shepherd; I shall not want." Such confidence could be heard in his voice that the audience rested in the assurance of the refrain "Though I walk through the valley of the shadow of death, I will fear no evil; for You are with me." Such peace flooded their hearts as he concluded: "Surely goodness and mercy shall follow me all the days of my life, and I shall dwell in the house of the Lord forever."

Silence engulfed the auditorium. The audience sat quietly, deeply moved by the power of God's Word spoken by a man who believed it. It was an awkward moment in the program. No one knew what to do next and didn't want to break the sacredness of the moment.

The young lawyer went back to the lectern to address the people. Looking across the faces of the audience, he said, "I want to tell you the difference between our presentations today. I indeed know the psalm. But that man knows the Shepherd."

That is the difference between being *spiritual* and being *religious*. A religious person knows the psalms, the creeds, and the catechism. The spiritual person knows the Shepherd.